WHEN IT CLICKS

Amitabh Pandey studied Economics at St Stephen's College and Delhi School of Economics. He taught at an undergraduate college of Delhi University and then joined the Indian Railways where he worked for twenty-four years, during the course of which he conceptualized, implemented and managed the Railways' online ticket reservation system at the IRCTC. In 2007, Amitabh shifted to the private sector and spent five years building business software. He now lives in Noida and writes full-time.

Also by Amitabh Pandey

Himalayan White

Himalayan Hazard

Love in Lutyens' Delhi

WHEN IT CLICKS

FIELD NOTES FROM INDIA'S E-COMMERCE REVOLUTION

AMITABH PANDEY

PAN

First published 2019 by Pan
an imprint of Pan Macmillan Publishing India Private Limited
707, Kailash Building
26, K.G. Marg, New Delhi – 110 001
www.panmacmillan.co.in

Pan Macmillan, 20 New Wharf Road, London N1 9RR
Basingstoke and Oxford
Associated companies throughout the world
www.panmacmillan.com

ISBN 978-93-86215-82-6

1 3 5 7 9 8 6 4 2

Typeset by R. Ajith Kumar
Printed and bound in India by
Replika Press Pvt. Ltd.

This book is dedicated to all those who helped make www.irctc.co.in a reality. These include the senior management and all my colleagues and co-workers at IRCTC, all the techies who worked on the project, those in the Ministry and elsewhere who helped and supported us, and all our customers who had the confidence to use our services and forgave the inevitable inadequacies that they occasionally faced.

Team effort, at its very best, is what made this project a success.

Pulling together, we can.

Pulling together, we did.

CONTENTS

INTRODUCTION

Electronic commerce as a completely new way of doing business – a new business paradigm, as it were – began in India in the early years of the new millennium and has grown explosively ever since.

This book is an attempt to share both the learnings I have garnered from having participated in the building of India's e-commerce revolution from its inception, and some reflections on the nature of this phenomenon in general terms and as it manifested itself in India.

The 'learnings' chapters are personal and anecdotal. There was a personal story to be told since lessons were learnt as part of an extended and very demanding personal-cum-professional journey. The 'reflections' chapters are necessarily formal, analytical and a trifle bookish. The reader is requested to bear with the stylistic difference which results from an effort to present as comprehensive a picture as possible of the ongoing e-commerce revolution.

Indian society and the Indian economy had been seriously deprived of modern communication facilities for more than fifty years after Independence. Electronic commerce, by definition, requires reliable electronic communication services, and these were primitive in nature and extremely limited in extent till the mid-1990s. Then, a major shift in policy orientation occurred, based on a fundamental change in the political ideology of the state, that enabled a communications revolution in the country and thus made e-commerce possible. A tightly controlled and strictly regulated economy was liberalized, controls on foreign investment were relaxed and foreign capital flooded in to provide services for which a strong market existed.

One major area targeted by private capital was electronic communication. Within a very few years, the communications scenario in India underwent a dramatic change as did the civil aviation space, to name the two most significant developments relevant to our areas of interest.

Chapter 1 examines these developments in some

detail and establishes how the conditions necessary for the emergence of e-commerce in India were created.

Chapter 2 details the single most significant e-commerce initiative of the early years: the launch of www.irctc.co.in. The Indian Railway Catering and Tourism Corporation, a fully owned subsidiary of the Indian Railways, launched a portal to sell railway tickets for reserved accommodation online. Against all odds and to the astonishment of a very large number of nay-sayers, the venture was a huge success. Having led this initiative and learned some very hard lessons in the process, the learnings have been documented as important items of contemporary economic history, in the hope that they may be of help to others venturing into the e-commerce space.

The IRCTC experience and, later, five years spent building business software in the private sector also served to provide – primarily through mistakes made – a hands-on education in the rough and tumble of software project management. These lessons are set down in Chapter 7 in the hope that others may not have to trip over the same obstacles.

Chapters 3 and 4 examine the issues in introducing e-commerce to a traditional bricks-and-mortar economy in general and the Indian economy in particular. Familiarity breeds a sense of security and the unfamiliar is frightening, especially if it involves radically different ways of doing business transactions. When personal monies are involved, safety usually comes first and experimentation and risk-taking are generally at a discount. Persuading an Indian customer to buy and pay online, instead of transacting with cash across a store counter, requires demonstrable advantages to offset the perceived risk of going down an unknown path. One such advantage is, of course, deep discounting. But it is crucial that the product being sold online be 'suited' to the medium – a computer screen instead of a shop window – and to the customer, who is used to physical rather than virtual shops. It is argued that, given the nature of some of its principal products – the travel industry-travel ticketing in particular – is logically the first area that e-commerce entrepreneurs would look at in the Indian context. The manner in which this came to pass, and how things evolved in India after IRCTC set the scene, is examined here. Of interest is the enormous expansion of the range of products covered by the e-commerce revolution as time passed and the customer became more familiar with the systems and processes on the Internet. The speed with which the Indian customer evolved and 'matured', the adaptive agility displayed in response to the new and the so-very-different, is quite remarkable.

Two case studies follow, illustrating the manner in which fast-growing, venture capital funded e-commmerce initiatives have established themselves, and analyzing their business performance on the basis of data available. These are important because, at the time of writing, these were the only two e-commmerce start-ups that had gone public and disclosed detailed performance data on public platforms. This is the only detailed, publicly disclosed hard data available for e-commerce companies and, therefore, critical for understanding actual performance issues. There also exist useful sample surveys, by the Internet and Mobile Association of India, of the Internet space, which give some idea about the 'broad orders of magnitude' relating to the industry as a whole.

Chapters 6, 8 and 9 attempt to present a perspective on the 'revolution' that we have witnessed from the mid-1990s and which is proceeding apace at breathtaking speed. They include some general theoretical reflections on e-commerce: its 'generic' tendency towards a monopolistic structure and its seeming disregard of the normal business focus on profitability; a look at issues that are important but go beyond commerce, especially citizen-state interaction;

and finally, an examination of the development paradigm within which the communications and commerce revolutions have occurred.

The conclusion identifies the 'fundamentals' that e-commerce must stand on, and looks at some recent developments and constructive ways forward.

PREFACE

MIDDLE-AGED MEN RESPOND IN diverse ways to midlife crises. In my case, it was an obsessive fascination with an emerging field populated with young entities: computers, computing, the Internet, and electronic commerce.

My generation, born in the late fifties or early sixties, did not have computers at home and in school; and not at college either, unless it was engineering college, which in my case it was not.

At the comparatively ripe age of thirty-eight, I touched a computer – an HP laptop, I remember – for the first time, hesitantly, tentatively; the unfamiliar is frightening, especially if it is expensive and belongs to your boss. I spent half the night loading Windows 95 and Microsoft Office, quaking in my chappals all the while. But finally it was done and I got a reassuring message from the machine. Apparently all was well with it and I could, if I was so inclined, actually use it!

My midlife adventure had begun!

But to keep to the storyline: I moved to Delhi in 1995, summoned by a former boss who needed executive assistance that, for some reason, he felt I could provide.

Ensconced in a room on the second floor of the Ministry of Railways, I managed access to a laptop and proceeded to familiarize myself with the machine, Win95 and MS Office, and the myriad charms of the Internet, unstable dial-up connections notwithstanding.

Having learnt a little about the vagaries of the Windows operating system and the MS Office suite, I decided to get an idea of the 'programming' space and proceeded to waste a great deal of money I could ill afford on 'computer training'. The year 2000 was approaching and many youngsters, bedazzled by stories of a glittering world of high salaries and foreign postings in the world of computers, were flocking to 'training institutes' to learn programming. Nobody told them the brutal truth that without an engineering/ maths-science degree all such training was just enough to aid a general understanding of the subject matter at hand; nothing more. I personally consider the 'computer training' boom of those days a huge scam run by so-called 'computer training companies' on the Indian youth. I took all sorts of introductory courses – programming languages, relational database management systems and the like – and got what I wanted: a general notion of the brave new world of computers. My various course-mates, however, were hoping for much more. Most had inadequate qualifications; many did not have even a science or maths degree and none were engineers. I wonder where they ended up; the training companies, of course, laughed all the way to the bank.

When 2001 dawned, my tenure in the Ministry of Railways was about to end and my fascination with the Internet had reached obsessive proportions. All of us had heard about Amazon and its compelling journey from garage to international stardom, the almost infinite possibilities inherent in the 'Network of Networks', and the host of emerging technologies that enabled all sorts of strange things on this mega network. In India, the Internet was slow and erratic and e-commerce non-existent. But the possibilities were immense and the most obvious one – selling Railway reserved tickets online – was right in our own backyard.

In mid-2001, I joined the Indian Railway Catering and Tourism Corporation (IRCTC) and began the most exciting, frustrating, and ultimately rewarding professional experience of my life.

During 2001–2006, I conceptualized and, with the active support of the senior management of the company and the unstinting efforts of a superb team of young enthusiasts, implemented an e-commerce platform to sell Indian Railways' reserved tickets on the Internet. The initiative met with enormous success and served to lay the foundation for the e-commerce revolution that followed. In 2007, having taken premature retirement from the Indian Railways, I joined the private sector as President and Head, eBusiness of a travel and tourism multinational, and built an e-commerce platform and application software for various travel businesses of the company. Investment in travel e-commerce does not yield profits in a hurry – witness the losses of travel portals in India – and profit-making mid-cap companies have no appetite for long-term investments. Hence, I was asked to make a foray into application software development and leave e-commerce, with its attendant expenditures, for 'later'. It was akin to waiting for Godot, and was an important lesson in the risk-taking proclivities of established profit-making corporates.

In 2012, I left the travel trade and took to reading and writing; a long-held ambition that has yielded this attempt to record the lessons learnt during a period of enormous effort, significant achievement, some frustration and bitterness and, in the end, overwhelming satisfaction.

1

LAYING THE FOUNDATIONS

INDIA'S MODERN GROWTH STORY, its breakaway from a low, slow and dull, though 'not disastrous' growth pattern of an overregulated 'closed' economy, began from around 1980. The growth rate more than doubled and, gradually, a 'new' India emerged from the ashes of the old, so-called socialist, economy. The start of this new growth paradigm came, surprisingly enough, a good decade before the economic liberalization initiated in the 1990s.

It has been argued[1] that the growth that began and continued through the 1980s was a consequence of a 'pro-business' shift in government attitude that focused on '.... raising the profitability of the established industrial and commercial establishments... Easing restrictions on capacity expansion for incumbents, removing price controls, and reducing corporate taxes (all of which took place during the 1980s).' In the 1990s, however, a 'pro-market orientation' emerged which focused on 'removing impediments to markets .... through economic liberalization' and favoured 'new entrants and consumers'. Trade liberalization, which occurred in the 1990s, is the 'archetypal market-oriented policy'.

Fascinating as the debate on causation is, for our purposes it suffices to note that the 1990s witnessed a high rate of economic growth conjoined with an opening up of many sectors of the economy to private investment.

With rapid growth as the background, the opening up, and subsequent explosive expansion of the telecom and civil aviation sectors, laid the foundation for the emergence of e-commerce in India.

The Communication Revolution

In India today, we take electronic communication for granted. Everyone has a cell phone and uses it incessantly, as do their grandmothers, cooks, and colleagues. Indians constitute, very probably, one of the biggest markets for cellular phones and related applications. It is, however, useful to remember that the communication revolution came to our country only in the mid-1990s. Cellular telephony, the Internet, and, with it, e-mail and other associated applications, are, therefore, fairly recent phenomena for the Indian consumer.

Those of us who have worked in small towns in the Indian heartland and have lived with manual telephone exchanges, had found even DoT landlines with automatic exchanges, subscriber trunk dialling, and, wonder of wonders, international trunk dialling, miracles of big city life!

In the early 1990s, I was posted to a small, sleepy, central Indian town from modern Mumbai and came face to face with the harsh realities of telecommunications in non-metropolitan India. During my three-and-a-half year tenure, the DoT phone installed in my home – as befitted a 'senior' officer – did not work, ever! The exchange was manual: you picked up the phone and waited for the operator to say, 'Number please'; you gave her the number you wanted; and you were connected to it. But, this was in the realm of theory. In practice, no operator ever picked up! To receive the operator's attention you had to be an important politician, an important businessman, or an important government official. Railway officers who did not control VIP reservation quotas did not figure in this list!

And then, around 1995, suddenly the Internet arrived, accompanied by Hotmail, cellular telephony, Personal Computers, and something called Windows 95. In the early years, cell phones were bulky and expensive, and call charges extremely high. Even rather senior civil servants were not privy to such exotic communication tools in those days. My first PC, an assembled device for which I took a loan from the Government of India, cost a little over ₹80,000 and was very high-end for its time: it had 64MB of RAM!

Another mindboggling development that turned our insulated communication-less world upside down was email.

You were with it if you had email and a casually stated, 'I've got Hotmail, have you?' was as powerful as wearing 'imported' Levis used to be twenty years earlier.

India, before the last decade of the last century, communicated via postcards, inland letter forms and, in dire emergencies, used 'trunk calls' that sometimes materialized and were always horribly expensive. Children who went abroad to study couldn't WhatsApp their parents when they needed money urgently; they had to write a letter, send it by Airmail, and wait many, many days for a reply. This last, I personally feel, was an excellent tool for imposing financial discipline on youngsters vulnerable to the heady temptations of a comparative study of the Jazz Bars of Greenwich Village on a Friday night!

But things changed around the mid-1990s.

In 1994, a National Telecom Policy was announced. Given below are some relevant extracts from the policy statement.

National Telecom Policy 1994

Introduction

The new economic policy adopted by the Government aims at improving India's competitiveness in the global market and rapid growth of exports. Another element of the new economic policy is attracting foreign direct investment and stimulating domestic investment. Telecommunication services of world class quality are necessary for the success of this policy. It is, therefore, necessary to give the highest priority to the development of telecom services in the country.

Objectives

The objectives of the New Telecom Policy will be as follows:

a. *The focus of the Telecom Policy shall be telecommunication for all and telecommunication within the reach of all. This means ensuring the availability of telephone on demand as early as possible.*
b. *Another objective will be to achieve universal service covering all villages as early as possible. What is meant by the expression universal service is the provision of access to all people for certain basic telecom services at affordable and reasonable prices.*

Present Status

The present telephone density in India is about 0.8 per hundred persons as against the world average of 10 per hundred persons. It is also lower than that of many developing countries of Asia like China (1.7), Pakistan (2), Malaysia (13) etc. There are about 8 million lines with a waiting list of about 2.5 million.

Resources for the Revised Targets

The rapid acceleration of Telecom services visualised above would require supplementing the resources allocated …

> *Clearly this is beyond the capacity of Government funding and internal generation of resources. Private investment and association of the private sector would be needed in a big way to bridge the resource gap …*

The Telecom Regulatory Authority of India (TRAI) was set up in 1997 to regulate this critical sector and new telecom policies were announced in 1999 and 2012 keeping in view the rapid changes in technologies, the growth of telecom infrastructure, and economic growth in general.

The point here is not to analyze the formulation of state policy in response to a rapidly growing sector, but to emphasize the revolution that occurred in this particular sector over the course of a short period of time. The fact that this revolution was enabled by a new emphasis in state policy on infrastructure and a liberal – some would say pragmatic – attitude towards private capital is significant and its implications will be considered in later chapters.

The availability of adequate and quality infrastructure facilities like energy, communication, and transport is a necessary condition for rapid economic growth, and the first serious transformation of the old India – many would argue the first of only two major revolutions, the other being transport, to date in this context – has been in the Telecom sector and all that goes with it.

A quick study of the telecom subscriber data, as available in the Annual Reports and other documents of the TRAI, is extremely educative.

The data clearly indicates that India experienced the start of a telecom revolution in the late 1990s. Before this the availability of telecom services was abysmally low but increased significantly thereafter, and witnessed explosive growth from the early years of the new millennium.

Teledensity (number of telephone connections per 100 population) in India in 1948 was 0.02 and rose to an inglorious figure of 1.94 in 1998. In the first fifty years of independence, we were seriously challenged, telecom-wise!

The situation began changing in the mid-1990s, but the telecom revolution really gained traction only in the new millennium.

Mobile telephony grew explosively as cell phones became cheaper and call rates fell drastically. From around Rs 16 per minute in March 1997, effective mobile call charges dropped to Rs 1 per minute in March 2006.[2] The Internet moved from dial-up connections that dropped frequently, to broadband connectivity. Incidentally, it may be noted that

Table 1: Telecom subscriber base (on 31 March)

Year	Teledensity (%)	Total subscriber base (mil)	Mobile/ wireless subscriber base (mil)	Fixed line subscriber base (mil)
1998	1.94	18.68	0.88	17.6
1999	2.33	22.81	1.19	21.59
2000	2.86	28.53	1.88	26.65
2001	3.58	36.29	3.58	32.65
2002	4.28	44.97	6.68	38.29
2003	5.11	53.91	13.00	40.91
2004	7.02	73.46	33.37	40.09
2005	9.11	93.63	52.20	41.43
2006	14.00	140.32	98.77	41.54
2007	18.23	205.86	165.11	40.75
2008	26.22	300.49	261.07	39.42
2009	36.98	429.72	391.76	37.96
2010	52.74	621.28	584.32	36.96
2011	70.89	846.32	811.59	34.73
2012	78.66	951.34	919.17	32.17
2013	73.32	898.02	867.80	30.21
2014	75.23	933	904.50	28.49
2015	79.38	996.41	969.89	26.59
2016	83.36	1,058.86	1,033.63	25.22
2017	92.98	1,194.58	1,170.18	24.4

Source: TRAI Annual Reports/Press releases
(**Note:** TRAI Annual Report 2012-13 states that for 2012–13 'the decline in wireless connections is mainly due to deactivation of inactive connections.' The report also mentions the fact of non- reporting of subscriber data by some service providers. This underlines the problem of some inaccuracy in subscriber data and comparability issues resulting therefrom. There are also occasional discrepancies in data reported for a particular year in different reports. For our purposes however, establishing broad trends is all that is required and the trends are clear enough).

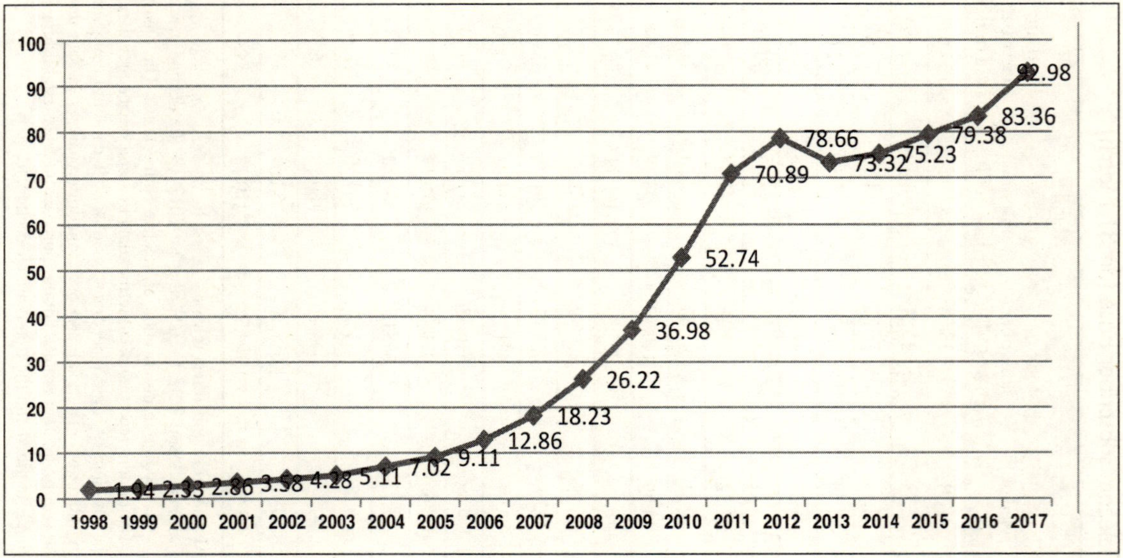

Figure 1: Teledensity (%)

broadband was defined in the Broadband Policy 2004 as always-on high-speed Internet access permitting a minimum download speed of 256 kbps! This was subsequently revised in July 2013 to minimum download speeds of 512 kbps! Performance is measured against stated targets and therefore it is important to evaluate targets before assessing performance.

Assembled PCs stopped costing the earth, home computing became a reality for the middle class, and children from relatively prosperous households began using computers at home and school. Television, too, benefitted from the economic liberalization of India in the 1990s and moved rapidly beyond Krishi Darshan to multiple channels and an enormous diversity of programming.

Despite a belated beginning in 1995, and a meagre 0.14 million subscribers in 1998, the number of Internet subscribers in India has crossed 422.19 million in March 2017, of which 400.62 million are, according to TRAI, wireless Internet subscribers. The bulk of 'wireless subscribers' are those accessing the Internet through mobile phones and the Internet revolution, therefore, is riding primarily on the mobile revolution. Between 1998 and 2006, the number of Internet subscribers grew strongly, from

0.14 million to about 7 million. Then, it exploded, crossing 164 million in 2013, 342 million in 2016, and hitting 422 million in March 2017.[3]

The pattern is now becoming clear: the communication revolution, which began in the mid-nineties, gathered traction in the early years of the twenty-first century and seriously accelerated from around 2006, growing rapidly, especially on the mobile platform.

The broadband subscriber base – a critical parameter for serious use of e-commerce and other Internet-based applications – grew from 0.18 million in March 2005 to 276.5 million in end March 2017 with a quantum jump after 2013. Though there were definitional changes in July 2013 which makes before and after comparisons technically difficult, we are not here concerned with exact values or any precise computations. Our objective is to establish broad orders of magnitude and the trends evident therein and that is straightforward and self-evident. Broadband subscriptions have grown apace since the inception of such services and growth has strengthened significantly from around 2014/2015.

It is important to note, however, that total Internet subscribers per 100 population, even in 2017, were

Table 2: Broadband Subscribers (million)

Year	*Broadband subscriber base (31 March)*
2005	0.18
2006	1.33
2007	2.33
2008	3.87
2009	6.22
2010	8.77
2011	11.89
2012	13.81
2013	15.05
2014	60.87
2015	99.20
2016	149.75
2017	276.52

Source: TRAI Annual Reports

32.86, while urban subscribers per 100 population were 70.83 and rural Internet subscribers per 100 population were 15.49 (TRAI Annual Report 2016-17). The bulk of India – especially in rural areas – is still significantly deprived of high-speed Internet connectivity.

It is not just Internet connectivity that is distributed unevenly. Even regular telecom subscription data, as the teledensity table below shows, betrays a strong bias towards urban areas.

Table 3: Teledensity: Rural and Urban (31 March)

Year	Rural	Urban
2015	48.37	148.60
2016	51.37	154.01
2017	56.90	171.80

Source: TRAI Annual Reports

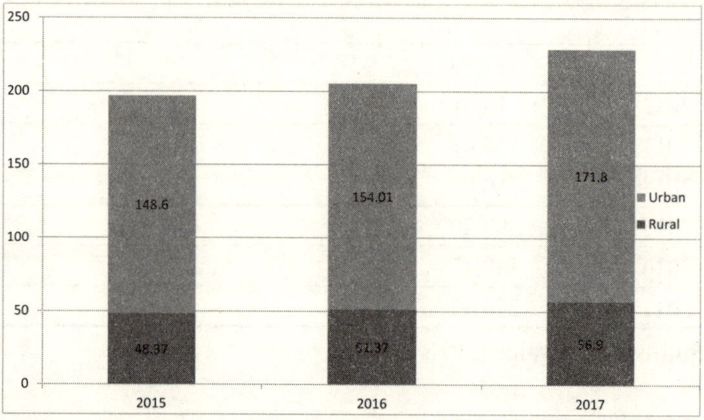

Figure 2: Teledensity – Rural and Urban

Source TRAI Annual Reports

This unbalanced growth highlights the urban–rural divide in the established pattern of Indian development and raises a number of interesting questions. The telecom revolution has been led primarily by the private sector. 'As on 31st March, 2017, the private access service providers held 91.06% market share of the wireless subscribers whereas the

PSU access service providers, had a market share of only 8.94%.'[4]

India's great leap forward from the 1990s has been attributed in large measure to the revolutionary opening up of critical sectors of the economy to private investment. Amidst all the self-congratulatory tossing about of high growth numbers, the issue swept under the carpet is that dreary one of distribution and equity. The free market looks for profit and therefore concentrates on areas of existing effective demand and if there is uneven distribution of income and wealth to begin with, the inequity will only get exacerbated by the flow of private capital. Growth, in our context, is necessary but not sufficient for equity and social justice, and telecom subscriber data seems to underline this rather vexed issue. We shall return to this issue later. Focusing on the e-commerce story, the one important point is that a whole segment of the economy – the rural sector – is still available as a potential growth area in times to come.

The beginning of e-commerce in India and its growth can now be mapped to the establishment and expansion of communications infrastructure and another significant economic phenomenon: the opening up of the civil aviation sector and the rapid growth of private 'full service' and 'low-cost' domestic airlines.

Air Travel Revolution

In May 1953, the Government of India nationalized the airline industry with the enactment of the Air Corporations Act, 1953. The Act created two corporations, Indian Airlines Corporation and Air India International, and the operation of scheduled air transport services was made a monopoly of these two Corporations.

In 1990, the opening up of the sector commenced with air taxi operators being allowed to operate in the sector.

In March 1994, the Air Corporation Act, 1953 was repealed, thereby ending the monopoly of the Corporations on scheduled air transport services. Domestic air transport services were liberalized and private operators were permitted to provide such services subject to a policy framework laid down to regulate the working of the sector. A number of private airlines began scheduled services including Jet Airways, Air Sahara, and Modiluft to mention a few. The 'low cost' revolution, however, came later, in the new millennium. Air Deccan, Go Air, Spice Jet and Indigo all started flying between 2003 and 2006.

In the Beginning

Chronologically, the pioneers in e-commerce were Ajit Balakrishnan with Rediff.com (1996) and Avnish Bajaj with Bazee (2000). Sify, listed in 1999, also participated in the early spread of Internet connectivity and introduction of e-commerce in India.

Rediff was never a pure play e-commerce venture. In its own words:

'Rediff.com delivers News and Information, Enterprise Email Services, Online Shopping Marketplace and Internet-based local TV advertising platform. These services are delivered on PCs, tablets and on a wide range of mobile phone platforms.'

Bazee was an e-commerce platform patterned on and later acquired by eBay, but it would not be inaccurate to state that in terms of sheer transformational impact on the Indian consumer and her mindset, www.irctc.co.in occupies pride of place.

A haiku* by Matsuo Basho is singularly apt here:

Spring too, very soon
They are setting the scene for it,
Plum tree and moon

---

* From *An Introduction to Haiku*, ed Harold G. Henderson, Doubleday & Co., 1958

The initiatives mentioned above did indeed set the scene for the e-commerce spring in India, which was inaugurated by the launch of the IRCTC's rail ticketing platform in August 2002.

IRCTC's online rail reservation platform was a runaway success, creating a much-needed acceptance in the minds of consumers of the reality and usefulness of e-commerce, including online payment. This has been IRCTC's most significant contribution. It initiated the Indian consumer into the mysteries of e-commerce and convinced her that it is actually rather simple, very safe, and enormously convenient. It served to change the minds of men and women – a difficult task in the best of circumstances – and got them to accept a whole new paradigm of commerce.

Close on the heels of the IRCTC phenomenon came the low-cost airlines. We now had a telecom infrastructure that could support serious e-commerce, as well as a business opportunity in the shape of private airlines that promised low fares and a jump in air travel numbers. This particular promise was fulfilled as can be seen from the data on domestic airline passengers maintained by the Directorate General of Civil Aviation (DGCA).

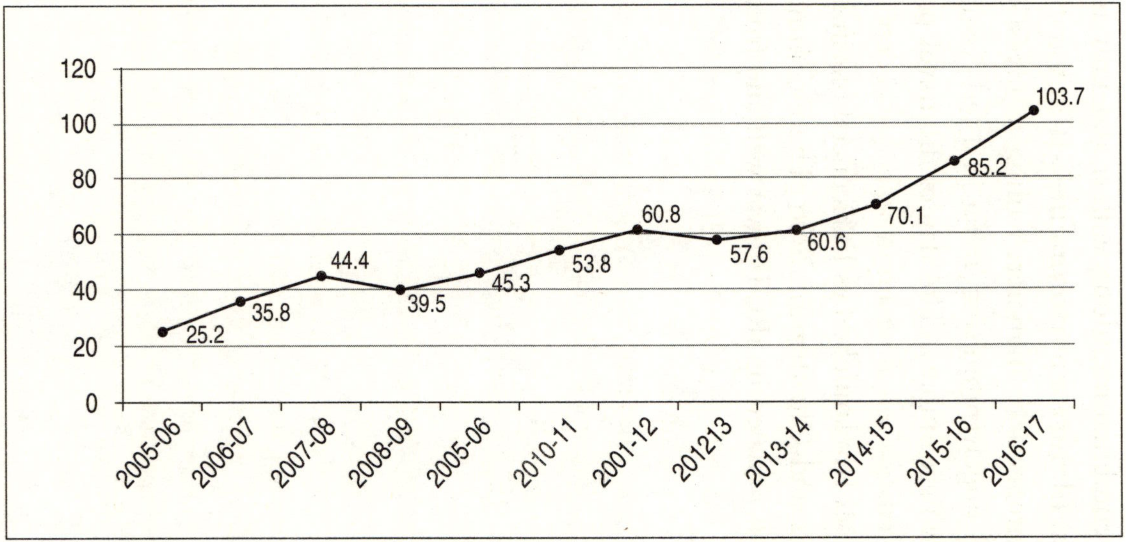

Figure 3: Domestic air passengers carried by scheduled carriers (mil)

Source: DGCA Handbooks of civil aviation statistics 2014/15–2016/17

This combination, along with a generally more open regulatory environment, attracted both entrepreneurs and financiers willing to invest in a new and hugely promising arena in a fast-changing and growing economy. The day of the travel portal had arrived.

MakeMyTrip launched its India operations in 2005 and Yatra and Cleartrip in 2006. The e-commerce revolution initiated by IRCTC was well and truly on its way.

2

THE IRCTC EXPERIENCE

THE INDIAN RAILWAYS – one of the largest rail systems in the world – has been a major driver of economic growth and social transformation since its inception in 1853. It can, in fact, be argued that the rapid expansion of the railway system served to make real, in an immediate, physical way, the idea of India as one nation, and was a necessary condition for the effective emergence of the nationalist movement in the late nineteenth and early twentieth centuries. The transformational impact of the Indian Railways (IR), both economic and social, stems from its sheer size. Large numbers of people from all strata of society – and large volumes of freight – travel by train for both short and long distances, and the IR network stretches across the length and breadth of the Union. Major happenings on IR thus have both a deep and a wide impact.

Table 4: A profile of the Indian Railways in the year 2016/17

Originating passengers carried	8,116 million
Originating revenue earning freight traffic	1,106 mil tonnes
Regular employees	1,308,000
Route length	67,368 kms
Number of stations	7,349

Source: IR Yearbook 2016-17

Sustained and gross underinvestment in capacity expansion and growing pressure on existing capacities have impacted the system adversely, but, in the field of computerization it has maintained a primacy that is often forgotten. The IR was among the first institutions to introduce mainframe computers for accounting purposes back in the day; more importantly, in the mid-1980s, the Railways 'computerized' the reserved ticketing system. What this meant was that while the customer still had to stand in a long line, fill up a paper form and hand over cash at a ticketing counter to buy a reserved ticket, the reservation clerk did his business on a computer terminal, not paper ledgers and registers. The Passenger Reservation System (PRS) that evolved was, and remains, a huge and remarkably efficient system – hardware, software, and networking – limited only by the technological possibilities of the time. Once the PRS was implemented and stable, the 'back office' of the reserved ticketing system was completely 'electronified'; a necessary, though certainly not a sufficient, condition for extending reserved ticketing services to the Internet.

The IRCTC Phenomenon

The website www.irctc.co.in was launched in August 2002 with the objective of selling IR reserved tickets online. Payment online was compulsory and the general opinion amongst the wise was that nothing much would come out of it; after all, who in India was going to pay online for anything!

The naysayers were proved wrong by the immediate and enormous success of the system, measured by its acceptance by increasingly large numbers of travellers and the huge increase in online ticket sale in a very short period of time.

To absorb the lessons from IRCTC's performance, we need to look at it from three different perspectives.

The month-wise ticket sale on www.irctc.co.in during the financial year 2002/03 is shown in Figure 4 below:

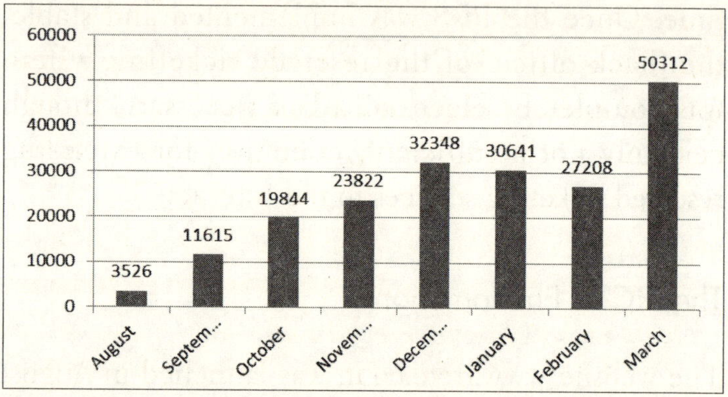

Figure 4: Ticket sales per month 2002–03
Source: IRCTC

Online ticket sale grew more than sixteen times in eight months from 3,526 in August 2002 to 50,312 in March 2003. Growth from a zero base usually looks more exciting than it actually is but this was, for the times, quite remarkable. The Internet was very new and rather fragile. Dial-up connections dropped all the time and made surfing a frustrating exercise, while making payment online was more or less unknown in India. In addition, the consumer was thought to be traditional and conservative and unlikely to adopt something as unfamiliar as online payments. Despite these rather adverse circumstances, ticket sales jumped within months of the service being available. The lessons here are simple. The Indian consumer is extremely savvy, weighs risks and rewards carefully and quickly, and is ready to abandon her supposed conservatism and adopt new commercial practices – including strange new payment systems – if the returns are considered worthwhile. The convenience offered by the IRCTC service was enormous and the consumer set aside her prejudices and fears and jumped right into the brave new world of e-commerce. Moreover, it may be added that the service proved itself to be a very reliable one; if one could book a ticket despite the limitations of poor Internet connectivity and problems caused thereby, the ticket – there were only paper tickets to begin with – was delivered promptly in almost every case. Refunds were processed very quickly by the IRCTC and this added to rapid consumer acceptance of the service. A brand was born.

If now we look at ticket sales over the first four years, we garner additional learnings (Figure 5). In the first four years, ticket sales grew from a daily average of 810 in 2002–03 to 7,051 in 2005–06 – a huge growth when we remember that broadband was

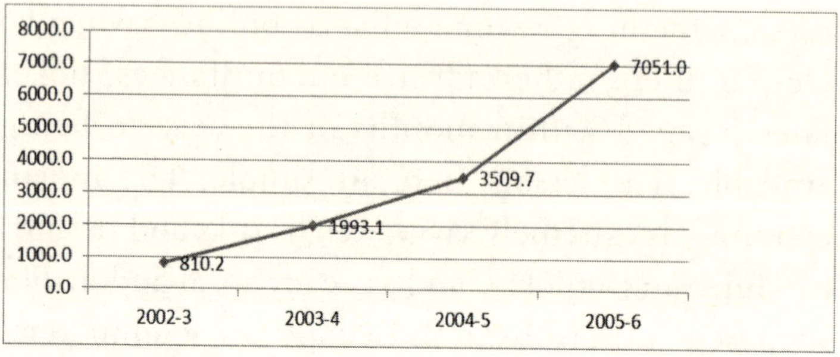

Figure 5: Average daily ticket sale 2002/2003–05/06
Source: IRCTC

still in its infancy in India, but telecom and Internet penetration – narrow band dial-up – were progressing rapidly. Despite the obvious lack of stable Internet connectivity for the bulk of Internet users, the demand for the IRCTC's services kept growing, and the IRCTC was able to meet that demand. Increasing numbers of Indian consumers were accepting e-commerce as a business paradigm. It is useful to recall that MakeMyTrip and Yatra began operations in 2005 and 2006 respectively.

A final perspective emerges when we step back and look at ticket sales from 2002–03 to 2017–18 (Figure 6).

Average daily ticket sales climbed from 819 in 2002–03 to 675,745 in 2017–18, which accounts for the bulk of IR reserved ticket sales (between 60 per cent

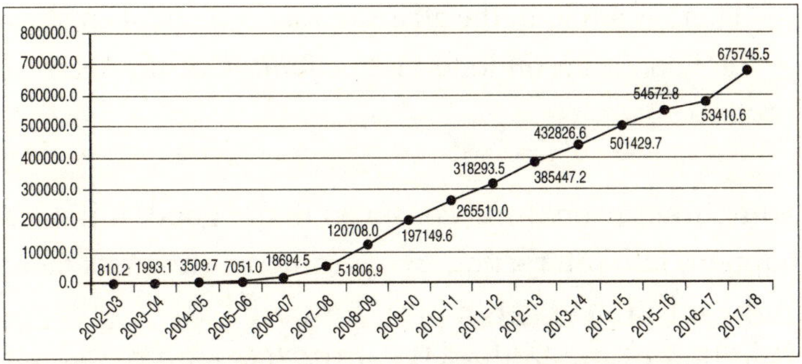

Figure 6: Average daily ticket sale 2002/03–2017/18
Source: IRCTC

and 70 per cent). The breakout occurred between 2006–07 and 2007–08 and was sustained for more than a decade. E-commerce in India during this period has grown beyond rail ticketing, first to domestic air ticketing and hotel booking and then beyond travel to just about everything under the sun. As telecom and Internet penetration proceeded apace, the customer accepted the e-commerce paradigm and private investment flowed into e-com start-ups, a decidedly new age in the commercial space in India took birth.

My personal involvement with the IRCTC ended in mid-2006, but the lessons learnt from that experience have stayed with me.

> 'There is a tide in the affairs of men which taken at the flood leads on to fortune' – *Julius Caesar*, Act 4 Scene 3

Sometimes everything conspires to the good: miracles happen, fate intervenes, 'synchronicity' shows its face, and your project gets a push forward.

When I went to the MD of IRCTC, and suggested that we build a system to sell reserved IR tickets on the Internet, I got the approval in thirty seconds along with a warning to not ask for any large sum of money. I was also directed to prepare a presentation for the Railway Board within a week, highlighting the principal features of the project and seeking the Board's approval for it.

This was the year 2001. The Internet had come to India but large e-commerce applications did not exist and the government had not caught the 'e-Services' fever yet. In such circumstances, asking a Ministry for approval of a strange, new project without any precedent in a critically important area like reserved ticket sale is asking, at best, for a study to be undertaken, a committee to be formed to review the results of the study and 'put up' its recommendations to a suitably 'empowered' group through 'proper channels'. In effect, it is asking for the project to be unceremoniously buried.

We, however, got the Railway Board's approval within seven days! This is a cold fact and I was so bewildered that I made a careful note of it.

This was a minor, or in my view, major miracle. It must be remembered that the Indian Railways was amongst the first government organizations to undertake computerization and a number of railwaymen had been trained in the use of those wonderful machines many years ago.

In government, decisions are all too often made on the principle of 'safety first'; personal safety, that is. If you do nothing, your pension is not impacted, but if you do adventurous things and something goes wrong you may have to answer for years on end and pay for your initiative with a ruined career or worse. A proposal to use the Internet where no one had done so earlier was asking for rejection if the key decision makers were not familiar with the real possibilities of modern computing and communication; and most decision makers – especially the older 'senior' lot – were not. People in leadership positions in both government and the private sector at the turn of the century did not have computers at home and school.

The brave new world of computing was something that they were largely unfamiliar with unless, of course, they had a science/engineering background.

And here came the miracle: the key decision-makers on this occasion were knowledgeable about computers, computing, and the potential thereof, and needed no convincing that the project was feasible and desirable. The two Board Members whose approvals were critical were both computer buffs and one had even trained as a programmer at one stage of his career in the Railways. So the decision was made that as long as the IRCTC bore any and all financial risks and expenditure, there was no problem in sanctioning a 'pilot' project. So it came about that the project was approved in seven days.

Thus, the first lesson I learnt in my foray in the Internet space was that sometimes, for a while, everything conspires to the good, and you speed along merrily, the wind in your sails.

And then you hit the doldrums, your mentors leave or retire, and the long knives come out.

'Why should they do this project, we should do it instead etc., etc...' was the oft-heard refrain, the old sarkari way of not doing anything and not letting anyone else do it either! Empires are jealously defended in Sarkar, as they are elsewhere, and woe unto him who violates the *lakshman rekha*s drawn by empire-building babus!

The basic lesson is an old one: windows of opportunity open rarely and for short periods of time; one has to grab them when one sees them.

As Mikhail Gorbachev famously said, 'Life punishes those who delay.'

> 'Hear now this, O foolish people, and without understanding; which have eyes, and see not; which have ears, and hear not' (*Jeremiah* 5:21)

To describe the naysayers in government as 'foolish' is strong Biblical usage. I would rather contend that mindset determines our capacity to see possibilities in extant circumstances; we see only what our mental-emotional predispositions permit us to see.

In nineteen years of fairly disparate work experience, I had learnt that consulting experienced people is often useful and so invited myself to lunch one day to a senior and highly respected officer's room. I described in some detail what I was planning to do, received some useful tips, and was then asked how the customer who booked online would collect his ticket.

When I replied that I planned to courier the tickets to the customer, the senior colleague was aghast. It would be disastrous, he maintained. A ticket was a money value document and could not be trusted to a courier, for heaven's sake! I argued that courier companies we would deal with would be the large, reputed companies who routinely delivered money value documents of much larger denomination than a railway ticket. Also we would have strict monitoring, penal clauses, and other measures, but my senior colleague was not convinced. 'You cannot trust anyone with railway tickets,' he maintained. 'Why take the risk?'

At this juncture I cannot recall even a single complaint of misuse of tickets by the courier agencies. In fact, one of the most appreciated features of the system we later launched was the speed and efficiency with which tickets were delivered, most often on the very next day after they were booked. The courier system of paper ticket delivery has worked extremely well, even though, with the advent of e-tickets, it is now relatively insignificant.

The solution was staring everyone in the face, but my senior colleague could not even see it as a possibility. The reason, if I may be permitted to use what I consider to be applicable 'pop psychology', is the government mind-set that cannot accept a system that *goes* to the 'customer' and delivers something to him. The *praja* has to come to the raja, wait in line and humbly collect whatever is needed. The state does not go the public. The state cannot 'convenience' the public; the state would have no *poochh* if it did not 'inconvenience' the public. It's all about mind-set. Solutions exist but are disregarded – not even noticed – because they violate the basic principles on which the state apparatus defines itself and its systems and processes.

The conclusion that mind-set determines choice of solutions/processes is not confined to government alone. I have seen remarkably similar rigidity in the private sector. The Head of a very successful business unit once brusquely brushed aside my tentative suggestion that we could try to sell some of his best-selling products through the e-commerce platform I had built for the company.

'My products cannot be sold online,' he pronounced definitively. 'Face to face interaction is required here. You stick to ticketing and stuff like that.'

A successful boat cannot be rocked, established channels cannot be exposed to channel conflict, control – even minuscule amounts – cannot be relinquished and the thought of credit being shared is anathema to a successful, well-established business unit! In a larger context, consider the case of online travel in India. None of the big travel companies – in fact, no established travel company, big or small – pioneered online travel in India. It was left to a former banker to collect some money and launch MakeMyTrip! The lessons I learnt about 'risk-taking', 'innovation', 'out-of-the-box thinking' and other fancy phrases that are all too often profaned in the private sector, shall be discussed a little way down the road.

> 'Full many a flower is born to blush unseen...'
> – *Elegy Written in a Country Churchyard*, Thomas Gray
>
> *or*
>
> 'Good help is so hard to find these days'

Once the Internet ticketing project was sanctioned, I went looking for a team to help me implement it. Recruitment from the open market is a long, tedious and often unsuccessful project in Public Sector Units (PSUs), so I made a few phone calls to railway colleagues and friends in Delhi, Mumbai, and Chennai. My request was to direct to me any staff who were interested in computers and wished to work on a computer/Internet-based ticketing project. I did not ask for technically qualified personnel; all I required was an interest in computers and a willingness to shift to Delhi on deputation to IRCTC, a small, new PSU. I was not very hopeful, but very soon a small trickle of young people began arriving at my office. A few Enquiry-cum-Reservation Clerks came from Chennai and Bangalore, one Goods Guard (yes, the guy you see blowing a whistle and waving a green flag from the last coach/wagon on a train) from Itarsi in Bhopal Division, and another Commercial Clerk from Delhi. Most of these youngsters had spent money on acquiring rudimentary 'computer' qualifications – MCAs from obscure institutions, mostly – and were very keen on working on a 'computer' project. The only bait I could dangle before them was that of training in the field of their choice. Financially, they would be eligible for the government salaries and allowances permitted for deputationists in a PSU; no big deal in any respect. They all agreed and joined up very quickly. In addition, we hired two retired 'reservation system' experts familiar with the vast labyrinth of reservation rules and regulations, who had also worked on the project for computerization of reservation in the past. This team formed a 'middle management layer' that interacted with the technical team on the one hand and the senior management team – my second-in-command and me – on the other and helped build, test, and launch irctc.co.in in seven months' time.

The lesson here was a critical one: managerial skill and success is a function of personal intelligence and personal commitment to the job at hand. Formal qualifications are not a necessary condition for either personal ability or effective performance.

I was, of course, lucky. The Indian Railways is a sea filled with all sorts of people and I found a few with the abilities and commitment that I needed. However, even in the private sector there are often dark corners where ability lies hidden simply because the concerned people are not articulate or aggressive enough to push themselves forward, and senior management is too busy to look into dark, unimportant corners and pull out potential performers into the light of 'main-line' operation.

Start-ups are Born in Garages

The IRCTC experiment began, not in a garage but in a section of a corridor of an old building with miles of rarely trodden, high ceilinged, dusty passages.

The Indian Railways had given us permission to connect to their reservation system, and to easily and securely do so we had to be located close to, preferably in the same building as, their system. We thus went hunting for space in a reservation office building, a huge old structure with high ceilinged large rooms, many of which were grossly underutilized. And here came the fun of being on the other side of the table when dealing with government: all requests were met with a 'no'. I recall a shouting match with a colleague who said he would do anything for me as an old friend, but nothing for IRCTC. I recall similarly virulent antipathy to all our efforts from most quarters within the establishment. I can only put it down to an atavistic reaction to any invasion of 'turf' and territory that characterizes all large organizations in both the private sector and government. For those unfamiliar with government, let me clarify that the IRCTC is one of several public sector corporations owned by the Ministry of Railways. It is thus not a part of the Ministry or its departments and you go on 'deputation' to the corporation from your department and become an 'outsider' for the length of time you remain there. In our case, we were interloping 'outsiders' shoving our smart-alecky noses into what was not supposed to be our business and trying to take over territory belonging to somebody else. Change, as some wise person said, is difficult, and the bigger and older the organization, the more difficult it is. And this again applies to both the private and the public sectors and departments of government.

Considerable effort at many levels led to our being allotted a short stretch of the corridor that extends across the entire front of the building which was rarely used because it led to nowhere significant. In any case, just beyond our allocated boundaries, entrances were available for accessing the building proper, so we were no inconvenience to anybody. We set up house, or more correctly, office, in the two rooms we created with partitions in the corridor: a small room to be the server room and a bigger one to be the operations room. The server room was just large enough to accommodate three server racks and one small communications rack. We were fortunate that all the 'techies' required to go into the server room were slim and agile young men; no substantial person could possibly have entered the room without serious risk to either the servers or the person himself!

The website, www.irctc.co.in, was launched in August 2002 and ticket sales grew from 3,526 in August 2002, to 32,348 in December 2002, 53,170 in April 2003, and reached 104,167 in March 2004. As is evident, we grew rapidly in an environment where e-commerce was unknown and online payments regarded with profound suspicion, as continues to be the case even today. Although it was the age of paper tickets only, e-tickets came later, we insisted on online payment because it was an experiment in e-commerce and we had no intention of diluting the experiment with compromises like cash-on-delivery. Besides, the risk of mischief, and refusal by customers to accept and pay for the product, was impossible to bear with a commodity like rail tickets.

The month on month growth in sales quickly drove home the realization that we would outgrow our corridor office very quickly. Remembering the old adage that 'nothing fails like success', we went looking for substantially larger office space, desperation and despair from past experience spurring us on.

As I've observed earlier, sometimes fate takes your side in seemingly impossible situations. It certainly did in our case and the form it took was that of an abandoned building within the reservation office complex. With enormous trepidation we asked for the use of the bare structure – it had just walls and a roof, and no doors, windows, or anything else – and were profoundly gratified when the powers-that-be agreed to our MD's urgent representations and granted us use of the building. My young colleague and only other executive – in sarkari terminology, officer – working with me on the project full time, transformed the empty shell into an office in record time. We shifted servers, printers and staff, net connectivity and everything else to the new office in just one stress-filled day, and although sales have reached the region of 7,00,000 per day at the time of writing about fifteen years later, that transformed old, abandoned structure remains the heart of the Internet ticketing system.

Question: 'Whose Baby Is It?' Answer: 'Nobody's!'

At one stage in the development process, disheartened by the persistent negativity from almost all quarters and especially from the 'Mandarins' of Information Technology in the Department, I asked a knowledgeable senior whether we would be actually allowed to complete our experiment.

'Won't they simply sabotage the whole effort technically and declare it a failure? Simple, really, if they so decide.'

The senior gentleman thought for a while and answered, 'They will not directly sabotage you. They know that you, and more importantly your boss, are rather passionate about the project and your MD is somebody the big bosses in the Railway Ministry listen to. He will create a major ruckus if there is direct sabotage and nobody has enough of a sense of "ownership" to take the heat that will come their way. A really strong person would have destroyed you, and explained away the mess as your failure, but there is no such person there. But don't think you will have an easy time either. They will do everything, short of direct sabotage, to discredit the project and your corporation.'

The words were prescient. There was no direct sabotage, but the negativity was relentless. I remember walking out of a tumultuous meeting where we were subjected to considerable humiliation and was told by my seething boss words to the effect that he had never in his entire career taken so much shit from anyone, let alone colleagues of his own seniority, as he had that day.

I remember replying with some bravado that I, too, in my considerably shorter career, had never let anyone get away with such behaviour without responding in kind.

It was a painful experience; but all of us, without anything being said, resolved to 'suck it up' and push forward. The best reply to all the opposition would be to make the project a success and smile politely at the opponents as we did so. All too often in life we come to a crossroads where we can decide to grow up and react as adults or 'flame out' in a blaze of personal ego and destroy a great deal of effort in the process. In very fundamental ways, the IRCTC project was a major growing up experience for me, though I was already well into middle age!

Samosas and Software Go Well Together

A crucial lesson learned during the development of the Internet ticketing application was that when the 'business team' and the tech team, or at least the 'tech lead', sit down together every evening for samosas and tea, good software is the result.

The practice of evening tea with our Chief Techie – a tall, thin, remarkably bright young engineer – started because twenty-odd years in the Railways had taught me that, *ceteris paribus*, results are delivered by teams, and team building requires togetherness. The team we had scratched together consisted largely of young persons from all over the country who had never worked together. So, every evening, I would summon everyone including our tech lead, order tea and the hot samosas that he loved, and we would sit together and natter. The conversation was generally about work – we were all a little obsessed – and a great deal of requirement refining and design optimization emerged from those sessions.

A fundamental requirement of good software development is the complete familiarity of the technical designer with the business processes and requirements. The designer must be immersed in the business process; he must be converted into a complete businessperson. Then he will know exactly what to design and the project will be successfully implemented; a conclusion that not all software projects reach!

A detailed discussion of why many software projects fail – because the technical team does not understand in detail what it is to do – will come later, but in the IRCTC case this was not a problem. Our entire team – a couple of retired experts in the reserved ticketing field, veterans of the PRS development project, and our young 'computer savvy' admin gang – had all the time in the world to educate our chief techie about the nuances of reserved ticketing, the rules and procedures with which we had to comply, the utilities required to manage things efficiently, and other details. Thus the tech lead understood in excruciating detail the processes, constraints, rules, and requirements governing reserved ticket sales.

To this he added his extensive experience with ERP systems and other business software development and the result was software that worked well.

An important point needs to be made here. In the real world of software applications, perfection is aimed at, but never actually achieved. The best one can hope for is an efficiently working application without any major gaps or glitches given the possibilities and limitations of extant technology. Having implemented it, you then work to improve it, to close gaps that time, hackers, crooks, customers, and other well-wishers bring to your notice. Eternal vigilance is indeed the price of efficiently working software.

A modern fable about government and software applications is worthy of repetition here.

A long time ago in a desh far, far away the raja developed and implemented a major application that was of great use to the citizens. There was rejoicing in the streets when the application was launched successfully and both the raja and the praja were happy. All was well and all manner of things were well for many years. Then the application's performance began degrading and soon became extremely poor. The people were very upset, but the old cynics said that nothing better could be expected from government anyway! That was the way life and governments were designed. One young babu, however, was very upset by this state of affairs. He was young and earnest and very proud to be part of the team that had developed and managed the application and so he sat down and studied the problem in detail. He then wrote up a comprehensive note on why the application performance had degraded and what steps were necessary to bring it back to a satisfactory level again.

He then went in search of the boss-in-charge of the application. The boss-in-charge was difficult to get hold of as he always had important meetings to attend outside office around lunchtime that required him to leave around 11:30 and return around 3:30 in the afternoon! However, the young babu persevered and one day managed to spot the boss-in-charge coming into office around 11 o'clock. He rushed into his room and proudly presented his three-page note.

The boss-in-charge looked at his watch impatiently, but sat down and read the note. Having read it through, he carefully tore it into four pieces and handed it back to the bemused babu. 'When you become my boss, you can write such notes to me. Till then, go and do your work, keep the application going as best as you can, and don't tell me how to do my job.'

The young babu's face fell and the boss-in-charge took pity on him and asked him to sit down.

'You are young and inexperienced, my friend, but you are a good worker, so I will educate you a little. Remember, we are honest civil servants and depend on our salary and pension to feed our families. If our salary, promotions, and finally pension were to be negatively impacted our families would suffer enormously. The secret of ensuring that such a horrible fate does not befall us is very simple: do nothing. Nothing that attracts attention, that has any great significance, because there are whole departments whose job it is to identify such people and ask them why they are doing significant things; what is their interest in actually doing something instead of pushing paper up, down, or sideways. They view such people with great suspicion and often stop their promotions or even their pensions. That is their job; they have to show how many pensions they stopped to get their own pensions! So, my young friend, don't ask me to upgrade the system, to increase capacity to improve performance. All those require expenditure and you never propose expenditure; someone is sure to ask why it could not be avoided and the work done without it. If any expenditure is to be incurred it has to be proposed from above and reluctantly agreed to by us after much deliberation and discussion. Never propose it yourself. Doing nothing has no downside in government, my friend; doing something always does. Now go away and prop up the darned system and keep it going as long as my term here lasts; I'm late for my meeting in the Ministry and must rush.'

Luck Matters, and Professional Commitment Can Sometimes Overcome Politics

The IRCTC's application had to integrate with the PRS in order to enable online ticket booking; and integrations, as every techie will tell you, are a tricky business, especially when required to be done with legacy applications using very different technical platforms.

Here we were extremely fortunate. The young 'tech lead' who was nominated to enable the integration by the guardians of PRS was not only an outstanding professional but also a committed one. Despite being fully loaded with his regular work, he took this additional task as a challenge. Instead of delaying – the hostility of some of his bosses to the project and its consequent low priority was no secret – he gave time to our 'tech lead' in the late evenings and the two young engineers built an integration in about three months that worked efficiently for years thereafter. Professional commitment and integrity does sometimes win over departmental politics. The best do not always lack all conviction!

Transparency and Honesty with the Customer is the Best, Most Effective, Policy

In the early days, we once had a technical glitch at the payment gateway end that led to a bunch of refunds not being processed. Since our refunds were normally processed within twenty-four hours, this was an anomaly that a customer's email brought to our notice. We detected the glitch, had it fixed and began processing the refunds on priority. But since the process would take several days, I resolved to send an email to customers apologizing for the delay and assuring them that the problem was now fixed. The payment gateway people – dark-suited bankers, as I think of them – insisted that the mail was unnecessary and that I not send it, but I did and the response was amazing: only one customer was indignant and angry; all others were understanding and forgiving. The incident was relatively minor, but the learning was significant. If customers are otherwise happy with the service, a glitch is easily forgiven if one is upfront about it and is seen to have taken effective action in the matter.

Beware the Dark-Suited Banker

Since we had insisted on payments online for reserved ticket sales on the Internet, we integrated our system with multiple credit card payment gateways – there were very few available to begin with – and with Internet banking systems of the few banks that had them at that time.

Dealing with bankers – from both the public sector and the private sector – was a remarkably educative experience, memories of which prompted me to label this lesson 'beware the dark-suited banker'.

When credit card payment gateways were integrated and Internet banking was being enabled as a payment option by integrating with every bank that had Internet banking systems, I remember asking a bunch of dark-suited bankers if they would allow use of debit cards for online payments. I still remember the polite amusement with which my naive and ill-informed suggestion was greeted. How can one expect a mere sarkari babu to understand the subtleties governing the provision of financial services! They patiently explained to me that banks would never agree to debit cards being permitted for online payments. If somebody had their whole bank account cleaned out by some cyber-crook, imagine the PR disaster for the bank! I would love to meet those wise worthies again – at stratospheric levels of the banking world by now, I'm sure – and ask them why the selfsame banks are offering wonderful incentives to customers for using debit cards online!

The lesson here was simple: you cannot trust the wisdom of the dark-suited bankers. The stirring events of 2008–2009 – especially the collapse of Lehmann Brothers and similar companies – have, of course, reaffirmed my strong belief that you have to deal with bankers in the same way that porcupines make love: very, very carefully!

This lesson applies particularly to integrating with bank technical systems. There is a natural tendency to be vastly impressed by the self-advertised strength, reliability and all-round wonderfulness of large banks; all that marketing money has to have some impact, somewhere! However, when one starts integrating with them, enormous caution must be exercised to ensure security because, like all systems, theirs too are not perfect and often have vulnerabilities that criminals can and do exploit.

When the Big Boss Shakes His Stick, Even Public-Sector Banks Take Action!

When integration with banks started, I, like a good civil servant, wanted the largest public sector banks to be on board too. With that intention, I spent a long frustrating day wandering around the huge building housing the headquarters of a premier public sector bank in Mumbai. I met some middle-level officers, none of whom showed any interest in either me or my proposal to offer their Internet Banking services to our customers. The IT department, to whom I turned in a last-ditch effort, commiserated with me, assured me that my project was very interesting, but they were far too loaded with work to consider any integration for quite some time. I admitted defeat and returned to Delhi.

A couple of weeks later, I received a call from one of the senior IT officers of the selfsame bank who had met me very briefly and dismissed me quite decisively, asking for an appointment the following day. The next morning, in marched a team of four or five executives from all concerned departments of the bank and requested immediate integration with IRCTC's system! I was flabbergasted and said so in no uncertain terms. I informed them that after their summary rejection of my overtures, I had approached a number of other banks and commitments had been made for a number of integrations. Their turn would now come after some months. I also asked, very sweetly, I remember, what had happened to make them change their minds. And then the story came out.

A rival bank had advertised on the front pages of a major daily the payment services being offered by them for online rail booking. The chairman of the bank, whose officers were sitting before me, had seen the ad, circled it in red and sent it down asking why 'we' were not providing the selfsame service. Orders were then issued post haste for all concerned to go to Delhi and initiate an integration exercise immediately. A tech team had been nominated and was awaiting the first set of documents from our tech team; and they would not take no for an answer. Since one does not say no to such a big bank – and we needed their huge customer base – the integration was done very quickly indeed. However, I must admit to a gentle glow of pleasure in, for once, being a pukka bureaucrat that day. I don't remember exactly what I said – something like 'will take your request into consideration, consult my team about their workload, assess the possibility of making some ad-hoc arrangements …' – but it was great fun saying it!

A simple lesson here: when the big chief shakes the stick, everyone takes action, even public sector banks!

Change is Not Impossible, Even in Huge Old Bureaucracies

When e-tickets were finally introduced by the Ministry, after extensive debates and much resistance from some within the establishment, I had dire misgivings. The Indian Railway system is humongous. To ensure that all ticket checking and other customer-facing staff were thoroughly familiarized with the concept and reality of e-tickets, stern instructions were issued from the Ministry to the Zonal Railways to run 'training programmes' and other exercises to spread the word about the new type of 'ticket'. My fear was that a lot of staff would not know about the innovation in time and a whole lot of passengers would be seriously inconvenienced when, instead of a standard ticket, they proffered a 'printout' to a disbelieving Travelling Ticket Examiner. A clarification here: the first step in introducing e-ticketing was to ask passengers who had booked online to carry a printout of the ticket sent online as the 'authority to travel'. Later, of course, they were asked to simply to show the e-ticket on their cellphone or laptop. To my surprise, there were hardly any instances of passengers being harassed on account of their e-tickets. If memory serves me right, there was just one case of a passenger being de-trained for 'ticketless travel' because he was carrying a printout and not a regular railway ticket. This was a singular tribute to the efficiency of the much-maligned Commercial Department of the Indian Railways. Once they decided to implement e-tickets, they did so across the length and breadth of India most effectively.

Even large bureaucracies can change, if they decide to! The problem is getting them to accept and internalize the need for the particular change.

Only the Front-End Matters

One day, after the Internet ticketing system was well established, I got a call from the Chief Financial Officer of a large, important, and well-known government Agency asking for an appointment to discuss online payment systems. I was flattered that we were considered significant enough to be consulted and promptly agreed to a meeting. On the appointed day, the Chief appeared with a large team in tow and I had a delightful time lecturing them on the nuts and bolts of online payment systems and their implementation: the problems, the solutions, blah blah blah! Tea and snacks were served and consumed and then the senior officer asked for directions to the rest room. With the Chief out of the way, I enthusiastically congratulated the second-in-command, a grizzled, elderly gentleman with a mournful look about him, on their obviously having completed the humongous task of computerizing the 'back end' database to enable online payment of citizens' dues. The gentleman shook his head slowly and said that the 'back end' was not computerized, everything was still manual and all records on paper! Only payments were being planned for computerization since the high-profile Head of the Agency was keen to announce that they too, had implemented online payments! I couldn't believe my ears and mumbled something about how on earth would they reconcile payments with amounts due etc. 'Manually, sir,' was the brief reply. The Chief came in at that point and the conversation took a different turn. The team left in due course and I never heard from them again. I do not know what they actually did but the intention was mind-boggling.

To be fair, governments, both state and Centre, have come a long way since; and today I pay my electricity bills to the UP State government online and it works quite well. The danger and the temptation, however, remain – given the e-mania in government today – of fashionable flimsy front ends being implemented without the dull unglamorous work of backend computerization being completed first.

Security Matters; the Unknown is Frightening

One of the major constraints on the expansion of e-commerce in India is the reluctance of the Indian consumer to pay online. This has resulted in the evolution of high cost payment mechanisms like cash-on-delivery, and costs have always to be paid for by one or other party to the transaction.

The common fear of online payments stems from the general perception that online payments are inherently insecure and hence too risky to adopt. Security issues have, therefore, to be examined in detail in any study of e-commerce and its possibilities in the Indian context.

Consider the case of online payment via credit cards. In the old days, the data required to pay online by credit card was the credit card type and number, the name on the credit card, the expiry date, and the CVV number on the back of the card. If these were submitted online correctly, the payment would go through. The obvious security problem here is that if anyone could get to look at your credit card for a short while and memorize the information, that person could use the data to pay online and you would find out only when the bill came in many days later!

The risk was high. When you give your credit card to a waiter at a restaurant to pay for your meal it is with him for a considerable period of time. I use this example because at IRCTC one significant point-of-origin of credit card fraud occurred at a well-known restaurant in South Mumbai. Those were the days of paper tickets and inexperienced cyber thieves and we sent our people and the very cooperative cyber-crime police personnel for a delivery and caught some waiters red handed! A similar experience occurred with a shop at a fashionable shopping arcade near Haji Ali crossing. Here, too, the shopkeeper was capturing customers' data – he obviously had keen eyesight and good memory – and was using the information to buy rail tickets online.

The answer to this security problem is simple and powerful. The data required to 'clear' an online payment by credit card should include an item that is not available on the physical card, such as a Personal Identification Number or Password that is essential for the payment to go through. Thus, anyone stealing the data on your credit card cannot use the information to pay online, as he does not have the PIN required to complete the transaction. The credit card companies – Master and Visa – had developed this security measure called Verified by Visa/ Master Card Secure, and IRCTC was the first e-commerce platform to implement it in India. As is evident from the way IRCTC's transactions have grown, the implementation of this 'two-factor authentication' procedure has not hindered transaction growth in any way. I say this because, years later, when the RBI made this process mandatory, many e-commerce honchos cried foul. They lamented that such 'customer unfriendly' measures would restrict e-commerce growth and should not be enforced. Fortunately for the customer, the RBI remained adamant and e-commerce has continued to grow at a heady pace!

The customer, it appears, is happy to accept the inconvenience of two-factor authentication rather than suffer the inconvenience of credit card fraud; as a regular customer on the Internet, I certainly am happy to comply.

As a merchant, too, in both the government and later, in the private sector, I was happy to enforce the inconvenience of two-factor authentication rather than suffer, and have my customer suffer, the inconvenience of credit card fraud and subsequent 'chargeback' proceedings.

There is a fashion in public policy, and swimming against the current attracts considerable negative attention. In this context it has often been argued that ease of doing business was paramount for e-commerce in India. I, respectfully, argue that ease of doing business cannot be allowed to significantly increase insecurity and susceptibility to fraud of the whole process; it would soon kill the business that it was allegedly meant to support. Besides, the principle constraint on e-commerce growth in India was lack of familiarity with this new way of doing business and an enormous suspicion of online payments systems, especially their security. Two-factor authentication and widespread understanding of the security it offers is essential for customer comfort and customer conversion and thus for the growth of e-commerce in India.

In February 2018, as per the RBI, there were approximately 36.9 million credit cards as against approx. 855.4 million debit cards 'outstanding' in India. When one considers that people with credit cards often have two or more cards it is obvious that debit cards and Internet banking are the payment methods that e-commerce players should focus on for growth. However, the fundamental problem remains: the consumer must have confidence in online payment mechanisms; she must be reassured that they are both secure and easy to use. This requires two-factor authentication to be both enforced and knowledge of its security implications widely disseminated amongst the transacting public. The latest American fashion (in our context, being customer-friendly at all costs) does not always suit the Indian climate.

3

INTRODUCING E-COMMERCE TO INDIA'S BRICKS-AND-MORTAR ECONOMY

THE INDIAN ECONOMY HAS witnessed rapid economic growth since the 1980s and a growing liberalization of the economy from the early 1990s. A communications revolution and a transformation of the civil aviation sector began in the 1990s and, as it gathered serious traction in the early years of the new millennium, e-commerce took birth and began growing very rapidly very soon.

For a developing economy with famously poor infrastructure and enormous poverty, this was pretty good going, demonstrating yet again that you can be clever and nimble and extremely quick to adopt and adapt utterly new things if they add value to you, regardless of an otherwise 'conservative' outlook both socially and commercially.

To introduce an utterly new business paradigm like e-commerce in a society and economy that has barely got accustomed to a functioning telecommunication system, it would be logical to pick up products with certain specific characteristics. These characteristics would include:

- Relatively low cost. (When experimenting with weird new ways of transacting and making payments you don't want to risk too much money, do you?)
- Strongly branded products with standardized and fixed product definitions. (Known products from known and trusted suppliers with no possibility of some smart crook palming off some junk and disappearing into the ether.)
- Products not requiring any 'touchy-feely' on the part of the customer or products where an approximation of the appropriate touch-feel experience can be replicated online.

Furthermore, to nudge the naturally reluctant customer – remember the unfamiliar is frightening – the e-commerce paradigm must offer some huge value add: enormous discounts or massive convenience as compared to the process of bricks-and-mortar purchase.

In the Indian context, one obvious product meeting all these criteria was railway tickets; reserved railway tickets, to be precise. These are relatively low cost, are supplied by the government as a monopoly, do not require any touchy-feely by the customer and, most importantly, the bricks-and-mortar purchase process was enormously expensive in terms of time and energy and travel cost; online purchase therefore offered enormous convenience.

When the Internet ticketing project was proposed, many of the naysayers contended that the Indian consumer was not ready to pay online and that, since we were insisting on online payment, the project was doomed to fail; there would be no customers. The pessimists were proved wrong because the product was such an ideal fit and the sheer convenience for the customer of booking the ticket online and having it delivered to them (by courier in case of paper tickets and by email in case of e-tickets), tilted the balance in our favour. The customer put aside her suspicion of online payments and her reluctance to adopt it and pulled out a credit card or used Internet banking and paid online.

In a very basic way, the effective implementation and management of the IRCTC online ticket reservation project laid the foundation of e-commerce in India: it pushed a conservative customer to adopt a totally alien method of commercial transaction and accept it as something useful, reliable and worth adopting for the immense value it added.

When our project took hold in the popular imagination and online ticket sales accelerated beyond all expectation, the enormous feeling of satisfaction that all of us at IRCTC experienced was due to the realization that the project – which honestly speaking, did not involve any rocket science, technically – had, none the less, brought about a fundamental change and established something new with enormous potential in our economy and society.

The important lesson here is that relatively inexpensive, straightforward implementations using easily available technology can have a huge transformational impact on both economy and society, if they are intelligently and effectively used to solve significant extant problems. 'Rocket science' costing a bomb is neither always necessary nor always sufficient to make a difference.

For introducing e-commerce in an economy like India, another low-hanging fruit – almost but not quite as low-hanging as rail tickets – is domestic airline tickets. While not as inexpensive as rail tickets, they are not horribly expensive either, and in all other respects have all the advantages of rail tickets: a standard, commoditized product, not requiring any 'touchy-feely' on the customer's part. The emergence of low-cost airlines happened in India between 2003 and 2006, and in 2005-2006, surprise, surprise, the travel portals – which would become standard bearers of the e-commerce revolution – emerged, selling primarily domestic airline tickets.

Yet another set of products 'suitable' for introductory e-commerce are books and standardized, branded electronics – laptops, cell phones, and the like – and, sure enough, in 2007, Flipkart was launched and started by selling books and subsequently graduated to almost everything else including the kitchen sink!

The sequence in which things occurred – rail tickets first, then domestic airline tickets, then books, electronics and everything else – was determined by the fact that the railways were ready for the Internet; reserved ticketing had been computerized in the mid-1980s, and the domestic low-cost airline revolution followed close on the heels of the launch of www.irctc.co.in. The airlines were, of course, Internet-ready and ticket sales could be put online by a travel portal with relatively straightforward integrations with the relevant ticket distribution systems. Once the ground was prepared by rail and domestic airline ticketing, the Amazon clones came online followed by Amazon itself.

E-commerce Over Time: What the Data Tells Us

It is useful, at this stage, to look at some numbers to get a more concrete picture of the development of e-commerce in India.

The Internet and Mobile Association of India (IAMAI) has done sterling service to the cause of e-commerce by conducting detailed surveys that give us a broad picture of developments in this new and rapidly expanding space. Comparing the results of the surveys published in 2013 and 2017 yields fascinating insights into the emerging pattern of e-commerce growth in India.

The share of online travel in total digital commerce has dropped from 78 per cent in 2006–07 to 70 per cent in 2009 and further to 56 per cent in 2016. Thus, while travel remains the single most important business segment in Indian e-commerce, its significance is declining markedly. In parallel, business segments other than travel are growing in

Table 5: Percentage share in total value of digital commerce

	2006/7	2009	2016
Online travel	78%	70%	56%
Online 'non-travel'	22%	30%	44%

Source: IAMAI Digital Commerce reports

importance with a share of 22 per cent in 2006–07, rising to 30 per cent in 2009 and jumping to 44 per cent in 2016.

Table 6: Components of online travel (percentage share in total value)

	2009	2016
Domestic air tickets	63.4%	40%
Rail tickets	28%	26%
International air tickets	3.7%	20%
Hotels	2.1%	9%

Within online travel, the shares of the erstwhile low-hanging fruit – domestic air ticketing and rail ticketing – are dropping as the bulk of these segments are already in the online fold. Growth is, however, marked in international air ticketing and, most importantly, hotel booking.

The declining share of online travel, and within it of domestic air and rail ticketing, coupled with growing shares of international air ticketing and hotel booking is indicative of a maturing of the e-commerce market in India. The easy game has been hunted down and now big game is being increasingly successfully pursued. In the travel trade (as will be discussed in detail in later chapters) the profitable segments are hotels and holiday packages and, over time, the travel portals are attempting to shift from low margin ticketing to these segments. The increase in the share of hotel bookings is indicative of a positive movement in this direction.

The jump in the share of 'non-travel' e-commerce in total e-commerce is also clearly indicative of a gradual 'maturing' of the market, a widening of the scope of this new paradigm of commerce and its joining the mainstream of commercial activity.

Within the non-travel segment, e-retail now occupies pride of place (approximately 80 per cent of the value of 'non-travel' e-commerce in 2016) and in this segment electronics dominates. Mobile phones and accessories, together with computing devices and accessories, constitute about 52 per cent of e-retail by value in 2016. Electronics are undoubtedly dominant! Apparel, footwear, and personal/healthcare products have a 20 per cent share in e-retail, while kitchen appliances and other consumer durables have garnered a 15 per cent share. The growth of e-retail has been particularly marked in the last five years, which coincides – with a small time lag – with the explosive growth of Internet connectivity in general and 'broadband' in particular.

Beyond e-retail, we have utility payments and online matrimony and classifieds and the relatively recent and as yet small emergence of food delivery, groceries, and online entertainment. Recent though many of these developments are, we must take note of their rapid growth. Even in times of relative scarcity of funding for new initiatives, some of them have attracted the attention and loosened the purse strings of big venture capitalists (VCs). The case of Zomato comes to mind in this context. Who would have imagined at the turn of the century that an Indian portal focussing on food reviews and delivery would not only grow in India but would also spread its wings beyond the nation's shores!

The learnings from this foray into data are straightforward. E-commerce is growing rapidly – at approximately 30 per cent CAGR – and is now moving beyond rail and domestic air ticketing to more profitable businesses which are growing very fast. Viewed from the product side, the market is broadening and deepening, and thereby tending towards maturity.

I have been careful to dilute the seeming precision of the data quoted above by a liberal use of the word 'approximately' because only two e-commerce players, MakeMyTrip and Yatra, are listed companies (MMT and Yatra are listed on the NASDAQ) and have to disclose a huge amount of performance and other data in the public domain. All others are privately held and are under no compulsion to disclose anything to the general public. IRCTC is, of course, owned by the Ministry of Railways. Detailed accurate data on all aspects of e-commerce is, therefore, simply not available. Reports are generated from samples surveys and secondary research and therefore 'broad orders of magnitude' are all we can aspire to, and we should have no illusions about this fact.

The term 'maturity' used in the context of e-commerce markets needs a little elaboration here. The first necessary condition of a mature e-commerce market would be its widespread acceptance as a means of doing business. 'Widespread acceptance' implies a high proportion of the potential customers should be actual customers and they should not just 'reluctantly accept' the new way of doing things but comprehensively embrace all aspects of it: processes, products, and payment systems. Given this rough definition we need to examine the extent to which widespread acceptance of e-commerce is reflected in the available data.

The Payment Problem

The principal constraint on the growth of e-commerce in India is the distrust of this new business paradigm in the hearts of many consumers. In particular, online payment systems were and continue to be viewed with great scepticism

As argued earlier, the best way of promoting growth of e-commerce is to enforce secure payment processes and educate the consumer about the security characteristics of such systems. 'Ease of doing business' is the new fashionable shibboleth being aired by wise persons in the media, but security is a much larger consumer concern and has to take precedence over 'ease of doing business'. Besides, the enforcement of two-factor authentication by the RBI does not in any significant way add to the difficulty of doing business but certainly improves security of online payments a great deal. The current fashion in policy suggestions must not blind us to the ground realities of consumer attitudes and requirements.

The reports on digital commerce of the IAMAI reveal a disturbing trend in the adoption of payment methods by consumers over time. In 2009, the preferred modes of payment were Internet banking/ debit cards and credit cards, whereas in 2016 cash on delivery accounts for 69 per cent of digital payments. This is unfortunate for the simple reason that it is a high cost solution leading to significant inefficiencies in a process that would otherwise be seamless, smooth, and quick.

When irctc.co.in was launched, online payment – via credit card or Internet banking – was insisted upon and, while over time new instruments were incorporated, the basic policy of online payment was retained. This, in fact, was what the naysayers, both within and outside the establishment, said would be the reason why the platform would fail; nobody would be prepared to pay online! Time proved the pessimists wrong and established the fact that the Indian consumer was ready to put aside her natural distrust of online payment if the perceived return from doing so outweighed the perceived risk. Perception, ultimately, is all! The convenience offered by the service was obviously enough to persuade the cautious customer to put aside her inhibitions and use the online payment options available. What is forgotten in this context is that we were quite reconciled to the fact that our venture was an experiment and our objective was to provide the most customer friendly and efficient system that we could, price the service cheaply, and hope that the customer found it worth using. In later years, when big money flooded into e-commerce start-ups, it appears that the pressure for sales and market share from venture capitalists made the start-ups very hungry and impatient. Instead of waiting for the organic growth of a consumer base willing to pay online, adding security measures to online payment systems and educating the customer about them, they sought to bypass the problem altogether by introducing 'cash on delivery'. The high cost of this 'innovative jugaad' – cost of cash collection and handling, cost of transactions repudiated on delivery – was ignored in favour of the sales numbers that would be generated and could be shown to hawk-eyed VCs. As a consequence, a singularly inefficient and expensive component was added to the e-commerce process. This serves to establish that the new age marketplace does not always generate least-cost, most efficient solutions and the new business paradigm 'market share now, profits later, maybe' brings with it some expensive baggage. As far as payments are concerned, the e-commerce space is evidently far from 'mature' and all interested parties, including the government, need to address this issue.

In recent times, the state has made efforts to move to a 'less cash' economy by encouraging the adoption of digital payments. The effort has been a general one aimed at all businesses, whether bricks-and-mortar or e-commerce. A number of digital payment platforms, mobile e-wallets in particular, have seen rapid business growth but whether this trend is sustained over time with the 'remonetization' of the economy remains to be seen. As far as e-commerce is concerned, the payments scenario for now displays little 'maturity'. Online payments systems are still not widely accepted.

The Problem of Geographical Coverage

IAMAI data indicates that e-commerce is confined to a great extent to the metros and 'large cities'. The top nine cities account for approximately 52 per cent of digital commerce spend and if we add the share of 'small metros', about 70 per cent of total spend is accounted for. It is important to underline here the 'approximate' nature of this conclusion. The broad picture is, however, fairly clear: e-commerce is still largely a big city phenomenon. The irony here is that given our humongous population and uneven distribution of purchasing power biased towards urban agglomerations, a handful of big cities can and do provide a huge market in absolute terms and the breakneck speed at which e-commerce is growing has been sustained by a geographically limited space and a limited segment of the population. The disparity in telecom and Internet connectivity between the rural and urban areas serves to reinforce this picture of unbalanced development. This larger issue will, however, be considered later. For now, it is clear that the e-commerce sector is far from 'mature' although it is growing rapidly and is already a veritable tsunami of Schumpeterian 'creative destruction'.

4

E-COMMERCE AND THE TRAVEL TRADE

WE HAVE SEEN WHY travel ticketing – rail and domestic airlines – was the first conquest of the e-commerce invaders. Given the significance of travel in e-commerce, a deeper study of this phenomenon in India is warranted.

The travel trade is traditionally looked at either from the point of view of products that are the major components of the business or from the point of view of the purpose of travel, which logically leads to a distinction based on the nature of the consuming entity.

Travel products consist of transportation products including Ticketing (rail, air and bus, domestic, and international) and sightseeing (car trips, bus trips, boat trips, et. al, domestic and international); boarding, lodging, and conferences (hotels, both domestic and international, arrangements for meals, and conferences) and holiday packages (combinations of some or all of the above products, domestic and international).

These travel products can be consumed either for leisure (by individuals/families and groups) or for business purposes (by individuals or business groups). The end consumers can, of course, be either citizens or visiting foreigners.

Table 7: The travel trade – a perspective

Purpose of Travel	Consumer	Products
Leisure	Individuals/Families	Transportation including escorted sightseeing and board and lodging
	Groups	
Business	Individuals	Transportation including escorted sightseeing, board and lodging, conference facilities
	Groups – meetings, incentives, conferences	

Since rail in India is a government monopoly and online rail ticketing was taken up by a Railways-owned corporate, the first private sector entrants in the field grabbed the air ticketing opportunity created by the emergence of private domestic airlines – some low-cost, others full service – and the burgeoning domestic air traffic.

The rapid growth of the economy generated demand for domestic air transport, and the opening up of the civil aviation sector enabled private investment to come in to take advantage of a huge new business opportunity. The domestic airline space offered a reasonably large market and, more importantly, a rapidly growing market. Domestic air passengers carried grew at about 9.89 per cent CAGR between 2007–08 and 2016–17.[5] Technically, the new airlines that emerged were Internet-ready and it was therefore relatively easy to put air ticketing online; and so the inevitable happened: MakeMyTrip started domestic operations and others followed suit.

The problem here is that airline ticketing, especially domestic ticketing, is a chronically low-margin business and the margins shrank as the low-cost paradigm took hold. Agents are easy to squeeze compared to airport administrations, oil companies, and airline pilots. In addition, given the chronic incapacity of venture capital-funded start-ups to keep a tight check on costs – remember costs include the California-style salaries of senior managers in e-commerce start-ups – we have a situation of rather chronic unprofitability of travel portals.

The model can be summarized as under:

A low-margin product with a large and expanding market is selected and sales begin.

The ground has been prepared in part by those who have gone before and sales growth and growth of market-share of the sole online seller is rapid.

Competition comes in; e-commerce is new, exciting, fashionable and dead sexy, and so beloved of the deep-pocketed venture capitalist. The market is expanding and the share of e-commerce in the total sale is also expanding, so everyone's market share increases. As Voltaire says in *Candide*, 'All is for the best in this best of all possible worlds'.

Ten odd years go by. Profits don't manifest themselves, but who cares? Market share is increasing and market share is God.

The infamous S-shaped curve now shows itself. The rapid growth of market share shows signs of slowing down and profitability still remains a distant mirage.

The next step is simple. Find another product

that can replicate – at least to some credible extent – the pattern of domestic ticketing and is also easy to implement online. In travel, the choice is obvious: hotel booking. Aggregators have emerged who have linked up electronically with hotel inventories and can offer to a travel portal technical 'integrations' that will bring to the customer a huge number of hotel beds online. Hotel booking offers better returns than air tickets and the field – online hotel booking – is empty. Every portal rushes into hotel bookings online.

Is this beginning to look like a sort of pyramid scheme? You make no profit for years on end despite rising market share and when the financiers may be about to get a trifle weary of the 'burn' with no end in sight, you dangle a new carrot – hotels will sustain the market share magic and also bring in some profit – in a while, of course, but sometime certainly.

Simultaneously, the portals gear up to get into the most profitable component of the travel business: packaged holidays. This is a very different kettle of fish, however, from the first two products. The most attractive area here is foreign group tours for Indians wanting to see the world in the comforting company of fellow countrypersons, with Indian food, Indian guide, and Indian prices. Unfortunately, group holidays abroad with family – we travel abroad *en famille* – are expensive and are bought from trusted providers; the portals are ticket vendors at best and one deals with a computer not a human being. You need to know the helpful lady behind the counter whom you can call in case of problems! You cannot get much reassurance from a call centre operative who you know is probably not even an employee of the portal.

In summary, successful holiday vendors have spent years building brands that customers trust. They have experience in building the right kind of product and managing it efficiently. The portals, by the very nature of the product and the customer, have an uphill task here. You cannot just plug in, discount and conquer the field. Besides, the established bricks-and-mortar players have strong brands, dedicated customer following, excellent products, and smart teams. The competition is strong, and market share is not so easy to grab.

In India today the travel trade has a few big bricks-and-mortar players making money from holidays (group and individual/family travel), corporate travel and MICE (Meetings, Incentives, Conferences, and Exhibitions), a whole host of mom-and-pop shops often making very good money from one or more of the above-listed travel products, and a handful of online players who have, for about a decade, been capturing market share in domestic air ticketing – losing money in various imaginative ways – and pushing into the hotels and holidays space aggressively if not necessarily very successfully, as far as holidays go.

So the question that arises is: What happens when the travel trade reaches this stage?

The core characteristic of e-commerce is that technology serves to obviate the need for physical, face-to-face, human interaction in a commercial transaction. The customer checks product availability online, selects a product online, and pays for it online. There is a fork in the road here. If the product is something that can be delivered electronically, whether a piece of software or an e-ticket, the final leg of the transaction is also electronic. If not, the physical product is delivered by the vendor and physical face-to-face human interaction occurs. Of course, when robotic drones begin to deliver products the human bit will go out of the delivery system too!

An interesting area for further exploration emerges here. To what extent can physical products be transformed into 'electronic' products that fulfil the designated function as well, if not better?

Reserved railway tickets were pieces of paper produced in secure printing presses to avoid possibilities of duplication, until the e-revolution transformed them into e-tickets that need not be printed at all! Perhaps one way of looking at it is that if the product (rail ticket) is not the final consumption item but merely an enabler to the consumption of some other service (rail travel on a particular train) then it is relatively easy to transform it from a physical to an electronic item. A few years of battling established mind-sets is all that is required. Let us, however, leave this theorizing to other minds and return to our subject: the future of the Indian online travel trade.

The extent to which online players can conquer the travel space depends on the extent to which they can successfully remove the human, face-to-face interaction from the sale/purchase process of the major travel products. They have already persuaded the customer to buy domestic air tickets online and are working on pushing her to do so for hotel purchases too. As they make inroads into the hotel booking space, they will, perhaps, control the losses they are making and also show increasing market share to their financiers.

Until they hit the 'holidays' barrier.

Consider the case of a family planning a foreign holiday and travelling on their own, not in a group. If they are planning a short holiday in a limited geographical area, are not fussy about food issues (don't need Indian vegetarian food all the time) are confident about their foreign language skills and not insecure about being alone in a foreign country (perhaps because one or more of them is familiar with the destination) they would probably do some research on the Internet and might even buy part of, if not all, the holiday components – air tickets, hotels and sightseeing services – online. To do so, they would need to be confident about making large payments online.

As is evident, we have managed to define a certain type of customer here. Such a customer is the natural target for an online player wanting to sell foreign holidays online. Such a 'sophisticated' customer, however, will shop around on the Internet: will look at multiple websites, including foreign ones; check with friends and relatives; and not just cling to one big-brand Indian online holiday vendor for all her needs.

So we have a possible problem here.

The 'sophisticated' traveller will buy the components of a foreign holiday online but is unlikely to exhibit any vendor loyalty. A growing economy and an increasingly sophisticated class of travellers – a 'natural' movement in an economy like India – will lead to increasing travel spend accruing to the online space in general, but not necessarily to a domestic travel portal. Remember: distance is dead. I can access an American or European travel portal, a London hotel's site and the Jet Blue and the RailEurope sites just as easily as a domestic one selling those products. In the online space, competition is worldwide. As the economy gets ready to buy foreign holidays online, it gets ready to try vendors anywhere in the world. Why would the traveller restrict herself to Indian travel portals?

This problem does not exist only in the domestic holidays space. If the person has reached a level of ease with the Internet and online commerce in general, she can be targeted by travel portals as a potential customer. Payments would have to be enabled offline and portals would have to have a strong trusted brand for holidays to persuade customers to come to them instead of to the established bricks-and-mortar vendors of holidays. Readymade packages may help here.

'Training' the consumer to buy at least domestic hotels online is a good first step towards persuading her to buy packaged domestic holidays online, but the transition may well take time. A bricks-and-mortar presence in the interim may well be called for either through franchisees or directly owned and operated outlets. Thus a 'convergence' may well be on the cards. It would take a lot of optimism and very skilful financier management to stay resolutely away from a physical presence on the high street and wait for the day to dawn when the bulk of Indian travel consumers are ready to buy at least domestic holidays online even if payment is arranged offline. In any case, a focus on domestic holidays appears to be called for; foreign holidays will definitely be more difficult to bring online in a hurry, and getting into that space will require major physical presence on the street, a drastic 'convergence'.

The situation is much worse in the 'escorted foreign group travel' space.

The product costs are very high, a great deal of payment is often in cash, and the bulk of consumers are not experienced enough to do away with the hand-holding that a salesperson in a shop offers. Most importantly, the transaction does not end with the sale of a product. The product involves physical escorting of groups of travellers from India to the destination abroad and throughout the tour and back! A sales transaction online – even if payments are arranged offline – is not the end of the matter. Portals have to develop the products, which includes planning itineraries, contracting with foreign transport operators and hotels, and putting together a team of escorting staff familiar with the destinations and how things work there. This is a far cry from plugging into a hotel aggregator's system and selling hotels to online customers. Bricks-and-mortar operators have spent years building up expertise and business relationships in this space, and have garnered a great deal of customer trust, goodwill and loyalty in the process. Breaking into this very profitable space definitely requires the online players to move towards a hybrid model of bricks-and-mortar presence in addition to an online presence. Building teams and expertise in this space takes time and effort as does creating a strong trustworthy brand as a holiday vendor in the customer's mind. This most profitable of holiday spaces is a serious challenge that technology and funding alone cannot help overcome.

In summary, travel portals must establish some offline presence to break quickly into the profitable holiday space. 'Convergence' is a necessary condition along with brand-building as a holiday vendor. The alternative is to persuade the VCs that the transformation of the Indian economy and the explosive growth of profitable online holiday sales is imminent, and until Godot arrives, capturing the hotels space and, of course, continuing the push into the independent travel holiday packages is the right course to follow. The successful emergence of pure play hotel booking portals serves to underline the fact that this is a business segment that is attractive. If a financier is tired of a profitless story he can always sell out; there are always other financiers.

5

MAKEMYTRIP AND YATRA: TWO CASE STUDIES

THE ONLY INDIAN E-COMMERCE players to get a public listing at the time of writing, have been MakeMyTrip (MMT), which was listed on the NASDAQ on 17 August 2010, and Yatra.com which went public in December 2016. As a consequence, we have 'hard' data – data placed formally in the public domain – for only these private players in the Indian e-commerce space. It is imperative, therefore, to look at their Annual Reports and other disclosures to get an authentic feel of the e-commerce paradigm as it has evolved in the Indian environment. While the data available for Yatra is not as extensive as MMT, an analysis and a comparison are educative.

There are other sources of information, amongst them the IAMAI studies and reports by some consulting firms, but other than the MMT and Yatra disclosures, they have necessarily to be based on indirect information and surveys whose sample sizes are limited. There are, of course, 'projections', guesswork, and media speculation to fill the gaps left by the lack of hard data.

MakeMyTrip

MakeMyTrip, founded by Deep Kalra, commenced operation in 2000, but for the first five years concentrated on inbound ticketing for the NRI market in the USA: US–India ticketing. They began their India operations in September 2005 with the launch of their Indian website.

We have reasoned that in a developing economy and society, which transitions from one with abysmal telecom infrastructure to one with progressively improved telecom facilities, e-commerce players would have to play a long-term waiting game. The potential customer would have to be educated about the possibilities inherent in this new way of doing business, the advantages to be gained, the sheer convenience of it all, and the checks and balances in place to minimize risk and maximize reward. The market would basically have to be created by seducing the customer who has three primary concerns: safety, convenience, and price.

The IRCTC played a major role in creating the market for e-commerce by demonstrating the enormous value that customers stood to gain: the sheer convenience of being able to transact from a time and place of one's choosing, and having the product delivered to one physically or electronically in a safe, time bound and efficient manner.

The IRCTC experience was, however, not enough to convince the consumer to transact online with other non-sarkari players for products other than rail tickets that may cost far more. The consumer had realized the value proposition offered by the e-commerce paradigm, but individual vendors would have to win the customer's trust for themselves. This required investment in establishing very efficiently functioning systems, especially the customer care functions, picking appropriate products – not very expensive and not requiring any 'touchy-feely' prior to purchase – and, most importantly, very 'competitive' pricing. Nothing excites a customer as much as a

Table 8: MakeMyTrip – an analysis (Fiscal year ending March 31)

	2008	2009	2010	2011	2012	2013	2014	2015	2016	2017
No.of transactions(in thousands)										
Air Tickets	1029.1	1250.8	1766.9	2824.6	3715.4	3794.1	3999.2	5432.8	6960.5	9379.7
Hotel bookings	36.9	81.4	109.7	175.9	343.1	568.1	869.8	1385.5	3137.3	6874.1
Net Revenue('000)$										
Air Tickets	14091.4	18733.3	31134	47622.7	66250.7	56769.2	62051.5	71509.2	76402	118514
Hotels and Packages	2365.6	5553.6	7995.7	10907.1	18226.3	27592.2	39992.9	62614.7	86449	140335
Other revenue	50.1	703.8	1152.8	2540.7	3707.8	3803.8	4350.7	4824.9	6169	14848
Total	16507.1	24990.7	40282.5	61070.5	88184.8	88165.2	106395.1	138948.8	169020	273697
Net Rev. Margins %										
Air Ticketing	7.1	7.2	7.6	7.4	7.9	6	6.6	6.1	6	7.7
Hotel and packages	8.9	10.6	14	11.5	11.9	12	12.6	13.2	15.3	18.8
Profit/loss($ million)										
Profit/loss	-18.9	-7.3	-6.2	4.8	7	-27.6	-20.9	-18.4	-88.54	-110.3
Dom air tkts txns		1200000	1600000	2600000	3500000	3400000	3500000	4800000	6200000	8600000
outbound air txns		45497	93757	146033	185623	241388	327392	463375	600000	800000
dom+outbound		1245497	1693757	2746033	3685623	3641388	3827392	5263375	6800000	9400000
Dom as % of total		96.3	94.5	94.7	95.0	93.4	91.4	91.2	91.2	91.5

large discount, and converting her from the secure and familiar pattern of going down to the shops to switching on the computer and fishing out the credit/debit card needed a powerful financial push. Cut-throat discounting was and remains a customer seduction/market creation tool.

An examination of MMT data will help validate these and other theoretical speculations and shed some light on the actual working of a large e-commerce player on the Indian scene.

While MMT offers a variety of travel products – air tickets, hotels and holiday packages, Indian Rail reservations, bus tickets, travel insurance, and foreign exchange – the bulk of their business comes from sale of air tickets and hotels and packages. In their own words, 'We generate revenue through two main lines of business, air ticketing and hotels and packages.' (Annual Report March 2017)

In the beginning, the focus was obviously on air tickets, but over time, a push to expand the hotels and packages business has evidently succeeded. The reason is obvious: the margins in hotels and packages are about double the margins in air ticketing (*see* Figure 7).

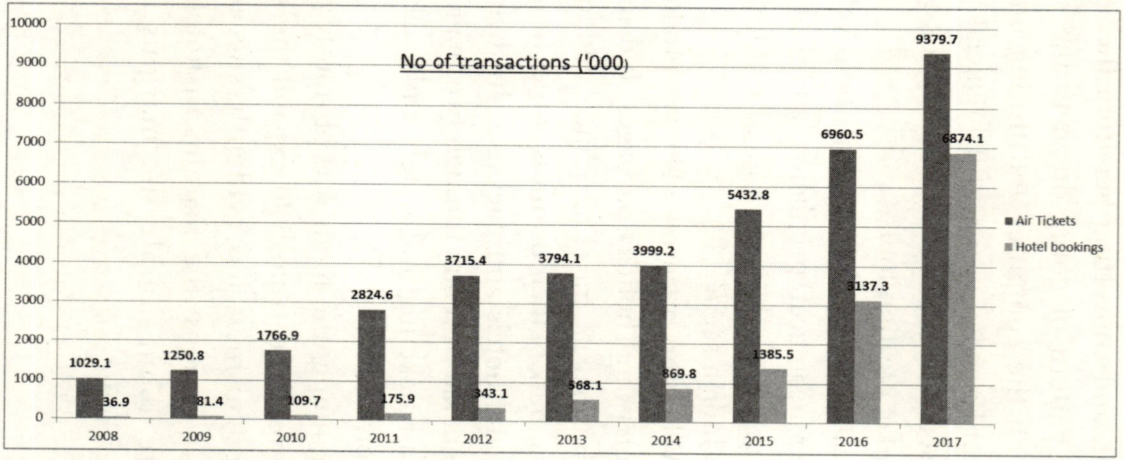

Figure 7: MMT Number of transactions ('000)

The picture becomes clearer when we look at net revenues:

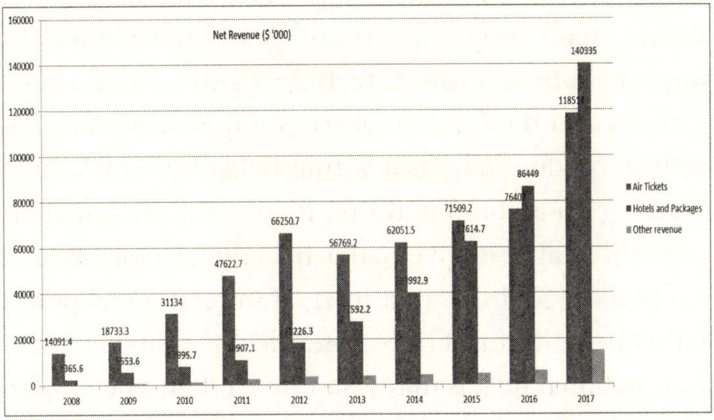

Figure 8: MMT Net Revenue ($ '000)

The earnings from hotels and packages have exceeded those from air tickets, whereas the number of transactions for ticketing are, in absolute terms, much larger.

Within air ticketing, the share of transactions for domestic tickets has drifted down from nearly 96 per cent to about 91 per cent over the last eight years, but domestic air travel still dominates the air ticketing business.

Domestic air tickets do not need any 'touchy-feely' interaction, are relatively low priced, and can be delivered electronically as e-tickets. They are low-hanging fruit in an environment still getting used to e-transactions and still suspicious of online payments. That said, the fact that international tickets are still a very small proportion of all ticketing transactions appears to be a business/technical failure both of the airlines and the Global Distribution Systems and the online vendor. Why is a young ticketing professional working on a command line interface with Amadeus or Galileo able to give better ticketing options than a supposedly sophisticated integration of a travel portal with the selfsame GDSs? Besides, the high cost of international tickets may also impact their sale online.

And so to the most important parameter for evaluating business performance: profit. Except for two years – Financial Year 2011 and 2012 – MMT has made losses in every year of operation and significantly large losses in recent years.

MMT's distribution strategy and the performance of different channels is educative. The company uses multiple channels for distributing their products: websites, call centres, airport counters in four Indian airports, company owned bricks-and-mortar travel stores (sixteen), franchisee owned travel stores (thirty-five), a network of approximately 3,191 travel agents across India who use their B2B website, and mobile service platform. (All data here pertains to March 2017).

During Financial Year 2017, 98.6 per cent of air tickets were sold on their website/mobile app. Hotel room sales were also concluded largely through the website/mobile app, but 'the majority of the sales of packages within or outside India are concluded through our call centres, travel stores and travel agents' network' (Annual Report for FY 2017). Furthermore, in Financial Year 2017, the mobile platforms contributed approximately 56.2 per cent of the total transactions carried out by the websites.

Yatra

Yatra.com started business in August 2006 – about eleven months after MMT – and went public in December 2016. Publicly available data for Yatra extends from 2015 through 2017 only, but a quick study of these three years does yield some interesting insights.

Air ticketing plus hotels and holiday packages are the two principal lines of business pursued by the company and the distribution strategy is a multichannel one: website/mobile app/agents (approximately 17,000)/call centre and bricks-and-mortar travel stores (twelve).

Table 9: Yatra's quantitative performance 2015–2017 ('000)

	2015	2016	2017
Air pax	4207	5698	6869
Hotel room nights	944	1139	1383
Packages-Passengers	100	130	143

Growth is evident in the data available but appears to be focused heavily on the air ticketing business. Given that net revenue margins are much higher in the hotels and packages segment, this pattern of growth is not very reassuring.

Table 10: Yatra net revenue margins (%)

Year	2015	2016	2017
Air	5.8	5.8	6.4
Hotels & Packages	11.8	10.9	10.8

When we examine the share of different product segments in the Net Revenue (Revenue less service costs) the problem gets highlighted even further.

Even by 2017, the company still has 70.3 per cent of its net revenue coming from Air ticketing and this share has grown over the last three years. The hotels and packages business is significant but its share in

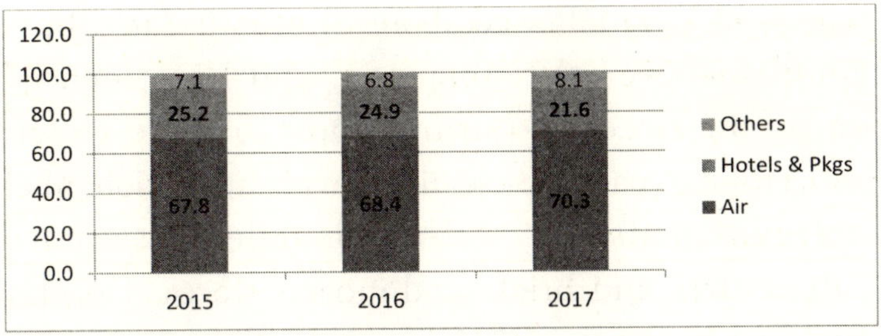

Figure 9: Share in Revenue less service cost (%)

net revenue has marginally declined from 25.2 per cent in 2015 to 21.6 per cent in 2017.

Losses have characterized the company's operations from the beginning and have seen a huge increase in 2017. While one year's performance may be due to exceptional circumstances, the overall pattern of Yatra's growth appears disturbing, to say the least.

Table 11: Financial Loss (INR '000)

2015	2016	2017
947,767	1,243,302	5,936,963
14.40%	14.80%	63%

Despite inadequate data, some interesting comparisons between MMT and Yatra are possible. Putting numbers aside for a moment, both started within a year of each other; MMT was first off the mark and Yatra followed about 11 months later. Both companies were VC-financed, and have focused on online ticketing (air/train/bus) and the Hotels and Holiday packages segment with a multichannel distribution strategy: websites/mobile apps/agents/call centres and bricks-and-mortar stores. Holiday packages have primarily been sold offline, giving rise to thoughts of 'convergence' over time with the bricks-and-mortar biggies who are busily building websites.

While MMT did show profits in two years and losses in all others, Yatra has not disclosed any profits at any time and the losses of both are large. Thus the two appear to be near identical 'clones'. The difference, however, appears to be in performance.

As the Yatra Annual Report for FY 2017 says '… we commenced operations with the launch of our Indian website in August 2006, and are now the second largest online travel agent company in India (as per management estimates based upon publicly available company filings).' While they do not name the first-ranked player, the status of being second is evident from the data.

Most importantly, however, MMT appears to have made the transition from grabbing low hanging fruit – low profit air ticketing – to building up serious business in the more profitable Hotels and Holiday packages space. (In 2017, Hotels and Packages contributed 51.27 per cent of Net Revenue while Air Tickets contributed 43.3 per cent. In 2008, the shares were Hotels and Packages 14.3 per cent, Air ticketing 85.37 per cent) This is a very significant strategic achievement and while acquisitions may have played an important part in it, acquisitions are a legitimate path for growth. Yatra, on the other hand, appears stuck in the low level Air ticketing segment. In 2017, the Air segment still contributed 70 per cent of Net Revenue and Hotels and Packages only 21.6 per cent.

As of now the race does not appear to be a strongly contended one.

The issue of sustained and heavy losses has called forth critical comments, especially from 'traditional' businesspersons. In response, however, it can be and has been argued that the need to 'create' a market and convert a very conservative customer to a completely new way of doing transactions takes time, effort, and lots of money. Capex is high because systems have to be state-of-the-art to ensure the best possible customer experience. Marketing expenditure is astronomical because a brand has to be created where none existed before and cut-throat discounting has to be offered to attract the customer, especially when a few equally well-funded competitors have entered the market and are doing exactly the same thing! Implementing a completely new and, to the customer, unfamiliar business paradigm requires burning a great deal of money over a long period of time. And besides, if the financiers appear not to be excessively bothered, why need anybody else be concerned?

Furthermore, since spectacular growth is essential to keep modern-day financiers happy and organic growth has its limits, acquisitions are called for and these are expensive. In addition, there is staff cost. Since high quality of service is essential, staff costs are high. If the losses of MMT are adjusted for employee share-based compensation costs, the losses would be very much smaller than they are. This is acknowledged in MMT Annual Reports and clearly visible in their data sets. Here again, if the financiers – or in the case of a listed company, the shareholders – approve, nobody else need be concerned.

All these arguments have a great deal of merit, but the emerging pattern is slightly disturbing. There appears to be a tendency towards a kind of hubris when large sums of money are available to burn. An attitude of 'Get me the best there is; money no object!' often leads to unnecessary expense, especially on technology and related services, that leaves the tech companies laughing all the way to the bank as they sell every 'state-of-the-art' thingamajig, essential or not, to a client who needs to say, 'I have the best' instead of 'I have all that is required at this point of time.'

Venture capital perhaps needs to do some introspection here. The excitement of breaking new ground and doing new things seems to have overwhelmed the old established rules of keeping costs under control and spending only on 'must haves' and not on 'nice to haves'. Since most VCs have their roots in the West or in Western oriented Eastern mores, and are used to dollar-denominated expenditures, the fact that a dollar goes a long way when converted to INR seems to be of little moment.

The two other significant patterns that emerge from a study of the data are: (a) customers buy tickets and hotel rooms through the Internet (websites and mobile apps), but holiday packages face-to-face from agents in shops; and (b) mobile commerce in products 'suited' for it – low cost, no 'touchy feely' requirement – is growing explosively.

These conclusions have important strategic implications both for travel portals and for bricks-and-mortar (B&M) travel operators.

One possible reaction from the B&M people can be, 'We told you so! The portals cannot compete with us in the most profitable segment of the travel business: the holiday packages business. We have long established brands, products and experience and expertise to create products that customers want. The travel market is immature; customers need a human face they can trust to sell them a good product and look after them if things go wrong. This is particularly important in the most profitable segment – foreign travel – where the less travelled person, who is fussy about food and unsure about his communication skills in foreign languages, needs handholding and prefers escorted group travel in which we are the best. A faceless call centre or website cannot meet their requirements in either group travel or independent travel.'

The reaction would, of course, be short-sighted in many ways. The portals have gained a dominant position in domestic air ticketing, which is not unprofitable, are making steady inroads in the hotel business, appear to be serious about the holiday business and are not shy about using offline channels to sell holidays either. They have established brands by spending a great deal of money and nothing stops them from making a serious push into holidays now.

The very Schumpeterian wave of creative destruction unleashed by the arrival of modern telecom in India and, with it, Internet and mobile technologies, threatens to wash away the sand castles of the established B&M players unless they take courage in both hands and invest seriously in the online space; in platforms, technologies and, most importantly, marketing. They already have brands so the marketing expenditures are unlikely to be large, but will have to be significant. Fear of channel conflict and reduced profitability in the short term – remember bonuses depend on profits here – must be set aside and effective online business established. Tokenism will not do.

As regards MMT, Yatra, and the other portals, if they can control costs, and the very natural tendency to look after themselves at the expense of everyone else, they may even achieve profitability. And if they can sustain the early 'fire in the belly' and ensure enough financing, they should drive into the holiday's space full tilt, like Guderian's panzers into a complacent, arrogant, and ill-prepared France.

The online travel agent start-ups came as business disrupters into the travel space and have aggressively built brands and grabbed significant shares in domestic air ticketing and are now moving into the Hotels and Holidays space. The few bricks-and-mortar biggies in the game – the bulk of travel is populated by small mom-and-pop stores – have yielded the 'low-profit space' without much of a fight and are clinging desperately to their strengths in Holidays in general, and escorted group international travel in particular, hiding their heads in the sand at the growing encroachment of the online players in the holidays space.

Consider an alternative scenario here. If one of the big boys in the bricks-and-mortar space, with deep-pocketed backers, bought out one of the big online players – not necessarily from amongst the first two, as there are other as yet unlisted players in the online space – they would be able to seriously give the portals a run for their money, or at least their share in the air and hotels business, and be for once in attack mode.

A scenario of 'convergence' and consolidation in the travel trade appears quite feasible and very likely at present: the portals moving into holidays and physical outlets to make that possible, and the B&M people doing something serious on the Internet. A 'hybrid' industry, using both traditional and modern channels with a few very large players, and myriad small mom-and-pop stores linked to one or more of the big ones, appears likely.

Regardless, given growing Internet penetration into rural India and sustained economic growth, the travel trade seems destined to live in interesting times.

6

SOME THEORETICAL MUSINGS ON E-COMMERCE

IT IS USEFUL TO theorize a little in an attempt to understand the nature and principal characteristics of e-commerce and the directions in which it is likely to move in any given business space.

A large city has multiple grocery stores because customer location is geographically scattered; distance is a critical parameter and many stores are needed to serve all customers effectively. Geography necessitates multiple vendors in different locations.

The telecom revolution and related developments like the Internet, accompanied by advances in transportation and logistics capabilities have, however, spelt the 'death of distance' in commerce. Geography no longer matters and location, either of the shop or of the customer, is irrelevant. A customer in NOIDA can buy a book from a portal hosted on a server in Canada and the book is delivered from a warehouse in the Mumbai suburbs.

Multiple stores are, therefore, not required to serve a large and geographically scattered customer base. Theoretically, one well-funded, efficiently run online store would be quite enough.

Another possible reason for multiple retailers in the same general line of business is product differentiation. Guptaji in Sarojini Nagar sells a higher quality of stuff, while Sharmaji in the same market sells a lower, more affordable quality of stuff and both remain happily in business. Here again, our ideal e-retailer with a large warehouse(s) in a cheap distant location can stock not only all possible products but also all possible varieties of each product; the 'long tail' in action. One retailer is again quite enough to fulfil customer requirements.

This leaves two major variables that can serve to differentiate between vendors: quality of service and price.

Standards of service quality are public and well-established and all well-funded well-run e-retailers would normally converge to a similar high level of service, or else they would go out of business.

This leaves only price as a means of vendor differentiation and that leads to heavy discounting by e-retailers.

Sounds familiar, doesn't it?

The e-commerce paradigm appears to lend itself, in a specific business space, to monopoly or at best – if the market size is large enough – to oligopoly with cut-throat price competition. A few sellers discounting heavily to grow/retain market share and thereby retain external funding and so survive appears to be the most probable outcome.

Two issues remain unanswered here: the issue of profitability, which in India is marked by its absence, and the problems arising out of limited competition.

As long as bricks-and-mortar retailers remain in play and the share of e-commerce in the total market size remains limited the evils of collusive action – such as price fixing – can be kept at bay. However, if oligopolistic e-commerce becomes the industry norm, these problems will automatically arise and will have to be dealt with.

The issue of profitability is more complex.

A newspaper some time ago highlighted the continuing Amazon–Wall Street honeymoon despite the sustained poor profitability of the former for almost two decades. Our home-grown travel portals have vigorously imitated Amazon in the poor profitability arena as have the more recent retail portals. This strange consistency is a trifle puzzling.

One possible narrative sold to financiers is as follows: India is a large market and, more importantly, the growth possibilities are immense. The consumer has just been introduced to the online space and will take considerable time to accept this new way of doing business. She has to be 'trained' to accept e-commerce, the infrastructure has to be built, the regulatory environment has to develop, and so on and so forth. A long transition period is inevitable. To reap the rich harvest of a humongous e-commerce-savvy market in the future, online players must play a waiting game which includes building state-of-the-art platforms at, it goes without saying, state-of-the-art costs, discounting heavily, advertising profusely and capturing market share in both the wallets and the hearts of consumers. Then when THE DAY finally arrives, discounting will no longer be necessary, profitable pricing will be implemented, the captured market share will nonetheless not be lost and immense profits will be made. Keep the faith strong, the wallets open and 'all will be well and all manner of things will be well.'

The questions that arise in response to this narrative appear rather simple, if not simple-minded.

- How long will the transition – and loss-making operations – last?
- Will the market share not be lost as soon as discounting is abandoned?
- Will bricks-and-mortar retail disappear? How come the huge malls that dot the US landscape still persist?
- Is the convenience factor of online retail applicable to all products and consumers for all times and circumstances? Or does it apply strongly only to some products in certain circumstances for some consumers?
- One can understand distant, small markets relying on e-commerce because their small local stores do not carry every product that they require. But such purchases will necessarily be small in number: consumers in a small village will order five flat-screen TVs in ten years.
- A trip to the mall on the weekend is usually a family outing; and not just in India either. Online purchase is not the most attractive option in all circumstances since outlet and other malls discount heavily too.

One possible response is that there are none so blind as they who will not see. If you lack vision you cannot appreciate the brave new world just over the horizon. Financiers are, reportedly, responsible adults and will choose the most convincing, if not necessarily the most correct, narrative from amongst those presented to them.

A final attempt at understanding the e-commerce phenomenon may take the following route: the computing and communication revolution and all new related technologies that have emerged therefrom are truly revolutionary and their transformational impact has just about begun to be appreciated. The potential for change is so immense, its depths so totally un-plumbed, that going by existing rules and thought processes in even something as mundane as the buying and selling of goods and services is silly. One has to jump into the darkness because there is a whole new universe out there waiting to emerge. Besides, in practical terms, the fraction of total investible resources dedicated to loss making e-commerce ventures is so small that it is well worth the while to take the chance.

The hungry eyes of the venture capitalist wolves may be dazzled by the glamour of the new paradigm of commerce that has emerged since the mid-1990s, but only a few of their irons are in this particular fire. The possibilities are immense, the risk in comparison, acceptable.

7

WHY SOFTWARE PROJECTS FAIL AND OTHER LESSONS

CONSIDER THE CASE OF a large bricks-and-mortar enterprise that decides to transform itself by getting somebody to develop software applications to run its various businesses.

First off, it hires a suitable IT person to do the job, unless it already has a small IT department, in which case it asks the existing IT person to do the needful. The problem begins right here. The applications are to be developed for the various businesses of the enterprise, but the baby is squarely dumped into the IT department's lap where it does not belong. The IT-wallahs, and any contractors they hire, are, in a manner of speaking, the midwife and mother-in-law; the baby belongs to the concerned business head who, however, neither acknowledges this fact nor takes much interest in the whole process.

There are several reasons for this.

In the first place the business head is a busy person, whose energies and attention are fully focused on running his business, getting the numbers for each quarter and the bonus at the end of the rainbow. He has no time for stuff that does not contribute to his primary objectives.

It also happens very often, especially in old established businesses, that there are well-established but not formalized, processes with a great deal of 'flexibility' built in. Computerization requires a detailed review, optimization, and specification of all processes; and that, in turn, requires enormous effort by the best minds in the business. And those minds are usually in short supply and fully occupied with the nuts and bolts of daily business operation! And so, the very first problem is the very basic one: what exactly is the application to do and how is it to do it? The 'tech lead' – the chief designer – of the application has to understand, in enormous, excruciating detail, how the business is run and what the detailed optimal processes are that he has to model in his design; and there is no appropriate person to devote the time required to educate him. For the sake of completion it must also be added that there are, all too often, vested interests in 'flexible' processes that are not fully documented. Computerization tends to put everything down in black and white and that can be quite inconvenient, on occasion!

The critical issue here is that the business heads for whom the application is being made must buy into the project wholeheartedly and commit time, energy, and manpower to make it succeed. They must accept the baby as their own and take full responsibility for it.

Regrettably, the baby remains an orphan in most cases.

The seeds of failure, at worst, or time and cost overruns, at best, are laid right here.

The action proceeds as follows: The project leader requests for meetings between the tech lead and the business managers and finds that the critically important managers are extremely busy – client meetings, suppliers' junkets to salubrious foreign climes, branch inspections, and what have you – and time slips silently by. When at last a meeting is actually fixed, the key business actors stroll in late, talking earnestly on their cell phones. Most of the meeting goes in the tech lead waiting with open laptop, the project manager grinding his teeth, and the business managers chatting on their cells. Another meeting is fixed at a suitable date several days or weeks later and the same drama unfolds again. When the Gods of Business do condescend to descend from the Olympian heights of their iPhones, they give off-the-cuff comments on the tech lead's plaintive queries and then nominate their juniors to fill in all the gaps. The least important junior is, of course, the only one who can be spared for the job. Months go by and some sort of specification requirement document is developed. A smart tech lead suggests that, before starting serious development, he would develop a set of dummy screens and show them to the business head and other important people to take their final approval for the application design and transaction flow. When the dummy screens are shown, the business persons react violently: the application is nothing like what they wanted; doesn't meet their requirements at all; and why is their time being wasted in this fashion!

The discerning reader would have guessed that the author has personal experience of the above scenario and she would be absolutely right. I remember marching into a CEO's room and announcing that without his personal intervention the project was doomed to failure. The CEO heard me out and then did a very carefully thought out *tandav*. He demanded that the business requirements gathering be completed within a fixed time period with back-to-back meetings between tech and business. He further threatened to attend the meetings personally and actually dropped in to a couple of them to drive home the point. The requirements were finalized in record time thereafter and I am happy to state that the application was successfully implemented without any further slippage.

While I have exaggerated a little for emphasis, the problem highlighted is a genuine one. Gathering the detailed requirements for software development is perhaps the most difficult part of such development. Business persons are busy people and adding to their workload creates major issues. The solution is obvious and enormously difficult to implement: the business has to put in a great deal of overtime on detailing the software requirements. Since this normally does not happen, even with all the goodwill in the world, in real life, software projects take a great deal of time to come to fruition.

The drama is repeated in slightly modified form a little way down the project lifecycle. When the application is considered ready for user testing, the project manager and tech lead proudly request the business honchos for a meeting to demonstrate their work and finalize the testing plan. The busy businessmen and women give a time, arrive late, talking on their cell phones, and the demo begins. Almost immediately a deadly disease manifests itself. It is called the 'Change Request' disease and is virulently contagious; it afflicts everyone very quickly from business head, through accountant, to sales person at the counter; often the chai-boy also has a point of view on the subject. It may be noted that the CEO has not seen the app yet. When he does, in the interest of leadership he will add his two-paisa bit, too. The 'Change Request' is exactly what it says it is: a request for changing bits of the application that should have been thought through and given as part of the requirements at the beginning of the project. To be fair, some changes are minor and can be effected easily. However, all too often whole new processes are thought of at this stage; major changes in procedures suggested by bright young – and not so young – things, whose capacity for creative thinking was dormant when requirement gathering was on and manifests itself only when the application is ready. The cure for 'Change Request' is as drastic as the disease. For every major change, the answer is 'NO'; the minor ones can be accommodated to smooth ruffled feathers and the major ones postponed to Phase II of the project. This trick soothes egos and ensures continued employment for both the tech contractor and the project manager! Sometimes, however, the request is made very cleverly: 'Yes we admit we slipped up and did not think of this at the time of requirement gathering. Everyone slips up once in a while, after all. Remember we are revising and optimizing processes and procedures to eliminate inefficiencies and loopholes in our working system. We are, in effect, building a new operating environment, not just replicating the old sloppy one and this new idea did not emerge then. But it has emerged now and has to be incorporated else the system is of no use. And you can go complain to the big chief if you like, we will suffer his wrath but still insist on incorporating this new idea.'

The answer here is: 'Sure, if you absolutely insist, but it will cost an additional huge sum of money and delay the project significantly, for which you have to answer to the powers that be.'

If they still insist, there is no option but to agree to the change and add as much as one can get away with, to the cost and time requirement!

Testing plans, like all plans involving the ultimate user, go awry with predictable regularity. The reason is the same as before: nobody has time for *faltu* work; everybody is very busy doing business and it's the IT department's baby anyway. Besides, in some cases, who wants a new system coming in and upsetting well-settled apple carts anyway?

Application development projects are doomed to time and cost overruns – it is an immutable law of nature. Incidentally, the IRCTC ticketing portal was developed, tested, and implemented in seven months and two days; an exception to the above rule, explained simply by the fact that the business owned the project and that the business manager and the project manager were one person and there was no running business to take care of. The entire focus of all of us business persons was on the application development.

The lesson is thus simple and powerful: business application development requires that the business own the development exercise totally. Then, and only then, can the software be delivered in reasonable time and at reasonable cost.

Deliver Us from the Dark-Suited Banker

A case in point here is when, in my private-sector avatar, I asked my team to integrate with the credit card payment gateway of a major private sector bank, one of the biggest in the country, highly respected, blah blah blah. I was in a hurry and was pushing the technical team hard and as a consequence we violated a basic principle: we believed the bankers when they said their systems were absolutely secure and the additional security measure we were insisting upon would be implemented, but not immediately, as they had some unspecified issues in doing so right away. We took them for their word and suffered a 'man-in-the-middle' attack resulting in a large 'chargeback' burden from a set of fraudulent transactions. That we caught the perpetrator ultimately and recovered most of the money is a happy footnote to an otherwise dark tale. In simple terms – the only terms I understand – a hacker placed himself 'in the middle' between the bank and our system and changed a set of bank responses from a NO to a YES. A set of credit card transactions that the bank declined appeared to us as transactions the bank had accepted and we provided the service to the customer. When payment time came, however, the bank declined payment as they had turned down the transaction. The integration mechanism proposed by the bank and accepted by us had a loophole that was exploited by the hacker. The selfsame loophole would have been closed had we insisted on the security mechanism we had demanded, instead of agreeing to postpone its implementation on the bank's insistence. We assumed, very wrongly, that the bank's stature ensured good and secure technology and we did not stand our ground on security issues and we paid for it with a very stressful six months!

To complete the loop, the security measure we had asked for, but not insisted upon, was a simple 'double verification' procedure that we had implemented in other integrations. The process is simple: when we get a response from the bank we open another 'session' and ask for a confirmation of the earlier response. Only when double verification is complete is the transaction allowed to proceed.

The lesson, fellow merchants, is simple. Do not hurry integrations, do not postpone security measures on anyone's persuasion and beware of the dark-suited banker!

Bank: '...if you integrate with us, remember, we are not responsible for any mishap under any circumstances, ever; even if our software is defective and technically we are at fault, remember we are not at fault and take no responsibility or liability of any sort....'

Merchant: 'Yes, sir, *mai-baap*, we agree most humbly; just allow us the privilege of integrating with you and paying you for it too...'

Anyone who has read a standard agreement that an online merchant has to sign with a bank to get online payment facilities – credit card payment, Internet banking – will understand the bitterness that tends to creep in when we recall the dark-suited banker.

When e-commerce was just starting in India, it is perhaps understandable that banks were very conservative about online payment systems. The technology was untested in Indian conditions and they really did not know how things would work out. They, therefore, made wholly one-sided agreements that in effect stated that under no circumstances would they take any responsibility or liability for any failures of any sort whatsoever; take it or leave it! Online merchants who had no option, signed those agreements and started business knowing that, in case of any payment problems they, the merchants, would shoulder all the burden of the failure.

Proponents of free market systems might like to consider the validity of a system where the monopolistic, rent-seeking financial enablers (money men, essentially) take no risk at all and the price of dynamic entrepreneurship is paid only by the direct entrepreneur.

The tragedy is that, even today, when banks have had many years of experience with online payments in India, the agreements they insist on are as blatantly one-sided as ever before and nobody raises any objections. The entrepreneurs are too busy building online businesses, and besides, cannot upset the money-wallahs if they want to remain in business, and the regulator appears to be just not bothered by such oligopolistic market imperfections. I am waiting for the day somebody revolts against this wholly inequitable situation and files a PIL against the dark-suited ones.

Some Words are Too Often Profaned ... in the Corporate Sector

In the jargon of modern business management, some words are used frequently and are all too often profaned. One such word is 'vision'. This quality, of possessing 'vision', is spoken of in hushed tones as one does about Nobel Laureates, for example.

Senior managers who deliver high growth in revenues and sometimes even in profits, are deemed leaders with 'vision'. What they are, in fact, are expert cost-cutters, successful hijackers of whole teams from competitors, able manipulators of Boards of Directors and clever stealers of large accounts from others. To be fair, they are also people who spot cost differentials between two countries, set up shop in the cheaper one and do scut work at cut-throat rates for the more expensive country: the 'visionaries' of Indian IT are a classic case in point. Testing software designed in California and making the GUI for it cheaper than they can do it in California is sound business policy, of course, but hardly 'visionary'.

To put it another way, in most cases 'vision' extends, primarily, to this quarter's numbers and this year's bonus.

Consider the case of e-commerce in India:

Bazee.com started operations in 2000 and irctc.co.in in 2002.

The 'low-cost' airline revolution was spread over 2003–2006 (Air Deccan, Spice Jet, Go Air and Indigo).

The travel portals started operations between 2005 and 2006 (MakeMyTrip India operations, Yatra and Cleartrip).

The whole e-commerce revolution – and it was indeed a revolution – began in the first six years of the new millennium, five years after the telecom revolution began in 1995 and brought the Internet with it.

If we recall that amazon.com started in 1995, we realize that the gestation lag in India was just five years; a tribute to the quick adoption and adaptation abilities of the Indian mind, both as entrepreneur and customer.

However, the important point to note here is that while travel ticketing was the low-hanging fruit to be plucked, none of the 'big boys' of travel ventured into the online travel space. It took stand-alone start-ups to grab the opportunity offered by the emergence of low-cost airlines, get some funding from venture capitalists, jump into the travel ticketing space and, very soon, capture a major chunk of the domestic air ticketing business. Their subsequent march into international ticketing and the highly profitable holiday space continues apace and the established bricks-and-mortar players cannot afford any complacence.

The point being emphasized here is that the 'vision' of established players in an industry extends primarily to the quarter's numbers and the looming annual bonus. Risk taking is at a severe discount, especially if it involves large investments with no immediate prospects of significant returns. They know that in the long run they will be retired and cannot compromise their retirement packages by huge investments in long-term projects with no immediate profit in sight. There are occasional exceptions, but they just prove the rule.

The much-hyped attributes like 'vision', 'passion' and 'out-of-the-box thinking' are conspicuous by their absence in the vast majority of senior business managers. Has anyone met a main-line banker who has ever taken a risk?

When you have something to lose you cannot afford to take a risk. It is only those who have nothing to lose – and time to make up the loss if they fail – who jump in where the fat cats fear to tread.

The cost of failure is very high in established enterprises. Which is why, 'breakout' entrepreneurship inspired by 'out-of-the-box thinking' is usually accomplished by outsiders to the industry in question, in 'start-ups' that have nothing to lose and the universe to conquer.

The Tale of Two Modules

The head of a major business unit wanted to develop an application for his business and made it clear that he needed no help except an introduction to the technical team developing modules for the other businesses of the company; he understood that the company had to use one platform for all applications. I introduced him to our tech partners and left him to it. Time passed and I carefully maintained my distance from that particular initiative until, at one review meeting, the CEO asked me rather abruptly why the module in question was not developed yet and why all accepted targets had been missed. I clarified, rather emphatically, that I had absolutely no idea as I was not associated with the effort in any way. I also emphasized, rather aggressively, that the CEO himself was well aware that the business head in question had not wanted any involvement of anybody, including me, in the effort which he was directing himself. The CEO grunted, moved on to other matters, and at the end of the meeting requested my presence in his room.

In the boss's room I was offered a chair, a cup of tea, and a simple directive: 'Sort out the mess in that project. It's delayed for far too long. I want that software implemented quickly.'

A good CEO keeps all options open. If a favourite does not deliver on something, the best way to take the heat off the favourite and also get the work done is to hand it over to someone else who will take the heat henceforth and, also, hopefully, deliver. In other words: find a suitable *bakra*! All CEOs are experts at this.

When you take over a messed-up software project, you take over everything and become answerable for it all. You cannot keep saying that the past was not your responsibility and the present is a mess because of the past and will take time to sort out. The bosses are not interested in history. You are in charge of the project and the project is a mess, so you are answerable for it!

In the case in question, there had been major communication gaps between the business and the tech team. They did not have samosas and tea together as they were located in different cities and communicated by email and telephone; and change requests were rampant, as the business had not thought through the detailed requirements before commencing development. The whole experience was a nightmare. Major changes in accounting were insisted upon a month before launch! The module continued to give trouble for years after launch.

The lessons are straightforward:

- Never accept someone else's mess to clean up
- If you cannot say no – not many can to a CEO – assess if the mess can be fixed and if not take a stand and insist on starting from scratch.
- Refuse major change requests or spell out the implications in terms of time and money. Being a 'team player' and taking on poorly thought out, poorly planned software projects is asking for very serious trouble in the future.

Remember the limerick:
'I sat next to the duchess at tea
It was just as I thought it would be
Her rumblings abdominal, were truly phenomenal
And everyone thought it was me!'

The tale of the second module is remarkably different. The business head had no ego issues tied up with the module's development and promptly agreed when I requested that she spend a great deal of time with the tech team, along with her best business people, and finalize the requirements after extensive deliberation. The requirements were finalized in a remarkably short period since the business head insisted on frequent and regular meetings with herself in attendance. The tech team was absolutely clear about what was required of them and change requests were minimal. It was developer heaven and the results were there for all to see: development, testing and implementation completed in record time and no complaints thereafter!

Seek and Thou Shalt Find People

In my private sector avatar, on a visit to Chennai, the regional head casually mentioned over a cup of tea that a 'very good IT person' was available in the Chennai office. The person in question was in a 'dead-end' job and looking for something more meaningful, but was not likely to get anything as he was very quiet and unassuming. I met Mr Bhaskaran for ten minutes, offered him a promotion and a place in the e-commerce initiative I was heading, if he was willing to relocate to Mumbai. He was and moved quickly and very soon established himself as a major pillar supporting the whole initiative.

Once again it was brought home to me that formal qualifications are simply not necessary for ensuring ability and effectiveness. I'm not sure if they are even sufficient; they are certainly more expensive!

8

BEYOND COMMERCE

THE COMMUNICATIONS REVOLUTION AND the accompanying development of Internet-based technologies have led to a lot more than just new ways of doing commercial transactions. In essence, processes for data storage, retrieval, access and communication have been utterly transformed. Data, and deriving therefrom, information and knowledge can now be stored in limitless quantities and accessed and retrieved at lightning speeds through modern communication networks across the globe. In this context too, distance is dead.

Every area that involved humans communicating with each other has been impacted and transformed:

teaching and learning, personal communication, medical consultation, expressing one's opinion, publication; the list goes on and on.

One area that has been impacted in a major way is the interaction between government and citizen.

It can be argued that in the transition from colonialism to independence, there were far too many continuities in the structure and, more importantly, the culture of the state and its institutions. Colonial institutions of state were essentially extractive institutions in a non-democratic structure and the culture was one of exploitation of the colonized people by outsiders with power, privilege, and entitlement. There were rulers and ruled, and the state used coercive power for maximizing the economic and political interests of the rulers.

If we step back and examine this description of the state we may be pardoned for considering the state institutions of independent India as little different in their functioning, from those of the colonial state. Somehow, electoral democracy has not succeeded in changing the manner in which state institutions function and those who man them comport themselves in their official capacities. The arrogance, the entitlement and the privileges continue, as do the exploitation and 'extraction'. The motive is not to protect and serve but to rule: to use power for personal aggrandizement.

Thus official human interaction with sarkari denizens has, in India, been a time-consuming, expensive, frustrating, and all too often, degrading experience.

Transforming the state and its functioning is a huge task even with all the good intentions in the world. The developments in modern communications, information technology and related commercial areas like payment systems can, however, contribute towards such a transformation. They can help as tools to empower the citizen and add to our society features of democracy beyond free and fair elections.

Information is one commodity that is hoarded jealously by an exploitative state and its minions. What exactly are the rules to be followed in a particular transaction with the state, what does due process consist of, what forms are to be filled and how, when can a particular functionary be met with, are some of the obvious questions that arise in any dealing with the state. A state concerned with 'conveniencing' its citizens, of empowering them, can use the simple tools of Information Technology to make available all such information in a comprehensive and accurate manner and ensure it is kept updated at all times.

This process of using modern communications and information technology to remove the 'sarkari human' from a citizen–state interaction has proceeded apace over the last decade and a half, beginning with the launch of www.irctc.co.in. Several state institutions have followed suit and made the citizen's life a little easier when it comes to dealing with government. The passport office, for example, has made an effective attempt to empower its customers and facilitate interaction with citizens.

Many transactions that earlier required physical interaction with a government functionary can be changed into purely electronic transactions, and an overworked, often rude and ill-informed and unhelpful babu can be replaced by an efficiently designed and well-functioning web site. The case of irctc.co.in is an obvious case in point. The fact that, in the long run, the government saves money by doing so is an added benefit; government manpower is amongst the most expensive manpower in India today.

The development of digital payment systems and their gradual acceptance by an increasing number of citizens has affected not only online commerce but also a huge area of state–citizen interaction—payment of government dues. Electricity and water bills even in Uttar Pradesh can now be paid online.

The days of queuing up at a bank counter for hours on end are over!

The fact that the state is willing to go online, remove its babu, and provide an electronic interface to the citizen is indicative of a welcome change in attitude. It does not of course transform the state into a caring, protective entity, but it is a good beginning that has been enabled by the revolution in communications and Information Technology. The cynical may contend that this is simply an example of the Law of Unintended Consequences. The technology came; people's expectations changed; the politician sought to impress the voter with 'new developments'; and, perforce, in some areas, the babu lost his little empire.

Questions of motivation are hard to answer but the fact of transformation of some areas of citizen–state interaction is undeniable. And once the genie is out of the bottle it is impossible to put it back.

The critical point here is that all such possibilities of eliminating direct human interaction in citizen–state relations be recognized and electronic interfaces be created and managed efficiently. This requires comprehensive computerization of data that lies in files and ledgers in government offices; a dreary unglamorous task that does not attract media attention or make for great PR. If, however, the effort is made, much of the citizen's burden of dealing with government will be significantly eased.

In recent months, government has made a huge effort to promote digital payments to bring about a 'less cash' society. The objective is laudable: convenience for customers, and visibility, and thereby taxability of erstwhile anonymous and invisible transactions, for government. The point here is that digital payments have not only to be safe and efficient but also seen to be so by consumers. Coercive measures are not the best way of changing long-held attitudes; effective education is.

If government can convince the customer about the safety and efficiency of digital payments, e-commerce too, would benefit greatly. The monstrous burden – high cost and inefficiency – of 'cash on delivery' would be removed and e-commerce would be hugely better off as a result.

In addition to forcing a change in the way in which citizens interact with government, the telecom and IT revolution has raised two new and serious issues that did not exist earlier.

These issues are: first an explosion in information availability; and second, the very real loss of privacy for anyone using these technologies.

Information overload is real and seriously problematic because it is hard to tell without significant effort how much of it is accurate and how much false. Because dissemination of information is easy and enormously fast, anyone can transmit false data in seconds across the globe. If one is plugged into the popular communication platforms of the day – one cannot be 'left behind' can one? – then one suffers this deluge of information and has to decide what to believe and what to reject. Image makers, data manipulators, marketers and other shadowy denizens of cyberspace use new technologies to push their agendas, some of which essentially aim at thought control through falsehood. The problem is real; the solution, not very obvious.

Another disturbing dimension of the technological revolution we have been studying is the huge potential it generates for loss of privacy for individuals. The technology that empowers and enables the individual in so many ways also enables a comprehensive invasion of your personal space by a 'big brother' who may be a Google who knows where you have been all day, or an intrusive government that wants to know who you have been talking to.

Technology creates possibilities and the exploitation of these possibilities is up to those who create, distribute, control, and otherwise manage technology and those who have coercive power to demand outcomes from the managers of technology: the state, for example. The nature of the state and how to control its natural intrusiveness is far too large a subject to be addressed here. Key words like 'national security' are all too often used to justify intrusion into citizens' private lives, because electronic intrusion is so much easier than the hard work of developing reliable sources of 'human intelligence'. An intelligence network that is efficient but not intrusive is hard to develop and maintain, whereas electronics provides comprehensive data – which has its own problems of validation – with much less effort. However, this too is not an area for exploration here.

All we need to accept is that there is a dark side of the Force that has been unleashed by the growth of modern telecom and Information Technology. How this dark side is to be managed needs extensive public debate and study.

9

THE LARGER QUESTION

WE HAVE SEEN THAT the Indian economy entered a new, high-growth phase in the 1980s and the state, in the 1990s, adopted an open, pro-market, liberal ideology and policy framework within which further economic development was to occur.

The opening up of hitherto closed sectors of the economy to private investment led to a revolution in telecommunication and related technological sectors, as well as in civil aviation, amongst other areas. Availability of modern communication and Information Technologies enabled the emergence of e-commerce in the early years of the new millennium with the Indian Railways – through the IRCTC, a subsidiary corporation – making the most impact with the launch of www.irctc.co.in, a portal for sale of reserved railway tickets on line.

The phenomenal growth of online rail tickets sale followed by domestic air ticket sales on travel portals and, ultimately, the emergence of Amazon clones and Amazon itself, seriously disrupted the retail space with the huge numbers they generated. In all the excitement of this development, the fact that this revolution was heavily biased towards the metros and the large towns was ignored, as was the underlying tilt towards urban areas in the spread of telecom services and Internet connectivity.

This imbalance is but one symptom of a much larger inequity in India's development paradigm and needs some explanation.

Relying on growth for development and, in turn, depending on 'open' or 'free' markets for growth has certain logical implications.

Markets focus on areas where effective consumer demand exists – actual or potential – and private investment flows into such areas to meet that demand and, if necessary, help create it. This logic implies that markets will ignore population segments and economic and geographical sectors where there is inadequate demand potential – in short, limited money in consumer hands – in favour of richer segments.

If we start with an unequal distribution of income and wealth and open up a 'closed' economy to the vagaries of the market, investment, and the resulting production of goods and services, will be aimed at meeting the demand of people who can pay for the products that they want.

Telecom and Internet connectivity, and services based thereon, have to be paid for. Those who cannot afford them cannot directly benefit from them. This does not take away from the value of these revolutionary new developments. It only goes to show that market-led growth has limitations in a society characterized by inequality in the distribution of income and wealth. If all are to benefit, the state has to intervene and enable those on the economic margins to participate in these new developments.

In the context of the telecom revolution in India this conclusion is reinforced by the fact that the states with the least teledensity in March 2018 are Bihar (63.12 per cent), Madhya Pradesh (66.99 per cent), Uttar Pradesh (71.21 per cent) and Assam (74.63 per cent). At the other end of the spectrum are the states with the highest teledensity-Tamil Nadu (134.11 per cent), Punjab (123.3 per cent), Kerela (121.61 per cent), Gujarat (112.44 per cent), Karnataka (109.01

per cent) and Maharashtra (108.46 per cent) (Source: TRAI Press Release of 23 May 2018).

The developed states of the Union show the highest tele-density and the traditionally backward states the lowest.

Whichever way we slice and dice the data, the conclusion is inescapable that the telecom revolution has favoured the urban areas over the rural and the developed states over the backward, thus exacerbating the inequities characteristic of the Indian economy from long before this revolution came about.

It is useful here to remember that, in the shadows beyond the high growth rates of the Indian economy, about 21.9% of the total Indian population lives in dire poverty (data for 2011–12) and this amounts to approximately 269,783,000 people!.[6] This number derives from a rather harshly defined 'poverty line', based on the estimated minimum consumption necessary for a human being. It must be emphasized that a large number of people not classified as 'poor' by this criterion will still be severely deprived of basic human necessities, and, thereby, the capacity to live with a modicum of dignity and fully develop their potential as human beings.

Rising tides lift all boats that are structurally sound.

They do little for boats whose bottoms have rotted away and which no longer have the capacity to float.

Tech revolutions brought about by 'free markets' will not directly eliminate poverty and inequality; direct state intervention is essential to achieve these critically important objectives.

The phrase 'effective state intervention' may be considered an oxymoron in the Indian context by the cynical but it is clear that growth based on the 'invisible hand' of a free market is not sufficient to ensure equitable development.

10

CONCLUSIONS

All business ventures must stand or fall on the fundamentals.

Convenience is the fundamental value addition that e-commerce offers to the consumer. This includes a huge range of offerings in one 'shop' – the 'long tail' effect – and home delivery of the product.

The convenience factor is particularly huge when the process of bricks-and-mortar purchase is markedly irksome, as in the case of rail tickets. It is also marked when availability in local stores is limited, say in small towns with no malls. Consumers who have very busy work schedules and cannot indulge very frequently in long laid-back shopping trips to the malls also find huge value in simply ordering online.

The market share and profitability of e-commerce should be determined by the convenience it offers to specific customers with respect to particular products.

The deep discounting that has become characteristic of e-commerce can continue only to the extent that e-commerce enables lower distribution costs vis-à-vis bricks-and-mortar retail. If this is the case, then, theoretically prices in bricks-and-mortar retail should fall to the online level and margins should become lower, resulting in long-term flight of capital and the ultimate closure of bricks-and-mortar businesses. The real world, however, has imperfect markets; besides, it is yet to be established that costs are lower in online retail. Discounting by online retailers thus becomes a strategy to 'educate' the customer, familiarize her with the brave new world of electronic commerce and capture her custom. When discounting – and loss leadership – stops, as it must in a rational business world, the portion of market share based on price differentials alone will disappear and the fundamentals – convenience in various forms – will resurface and drive market share and profitability.

Until that day dawns, and VCs remember the currently unfashionable notion of profitability, online retailers will continue to cut their throats and customers shall make hay in the sunshine of competitive discounting.

Recent developments in the Indian e-commerce space are likely to strengthen the possibility of this outcome. Walmart has bought a controlling stake in Flipkart and we now have two humongous US-based multinational retailers head-to-head in the Indian retail space. As far as we customers are concerned, it's 'Oh happy day!'

Some disquiet has been evident amongst the traditional bricks-and-mortar retailers about the emergence of such large online players and the likelihood of 'competitive discounting' to capture market share. If the powers-that-be can set aside the compulsion to protect traditional political constituencies, they should see that oligopoly is a natural tendency – part of the DNA – in the e-commerce space. Furthermore, beyond a handful of large online retailers there is space for the traditional small *nukkad ki dukaan* too. The small trader is clever and nimble enough and has already begun to find effective ways to survive and prosper in a world where e-commerce is growing rapidly.

The wave of creative destruction cannot, and should not, be held back to protect a constituency that has perforce to change in the light of modern developments in technology and business practice. The problem here is the old one of a well-organized constituency (small bricks-and-mortar traders) being politically more powerful than a much, much larger constituency (the general consumer) that is not organized at all.

It is to be hoped that in the context of e-commerce, policy makers will set aside the compulsions of politics and focus on the greatest good of the greatest number.

NOTES

1. Rodrik, Dani and Arvind Subramanian. 2005. 'From "Hindu Growth" to Productivity Surge: The Mystery of the Indian Growth Transition'. IMF Staff Papers 52: 2. All quotations in this paragraph are from this article.
2. Source: TRAI* Document 'A journey towards excellence in Telecommunications 1997–2007'.
3. Data collated from TRAI* documents – Annual Reports/Press releases etc.
4. TRAI* Annual Report 2016–17.
5. DGCA Handbook on Civil Aviation Statistics.
6. Source: RBI Handbook of Statistics on the Indian Economy 2016–17.

* TRAI sourced subscription data when quoted for a year, pertain to the last day of the financial year, that is, subscription as on 31 March.

ACKNOWLEDGEMENTS

My agent Preeti Gill, my editor Teesta Guha Sarkar, and my wife Sandhya Pandey (both critic and first editor) are responsible for this book seeing the light of day. Despite their best efforts, inadequacies remain, for which I am solely responsible.

The IRCTC Internet ticketing project was the most significant landmark in my professional life. This project would not have got off the ground and would have remained just a fanciful and unimplemented idea had Mr M. N. Chopra – then Managing Director of IRCTC – not approved and supported it at all times.

Thank you, sir, for everything.